URBAN CHINA

URBAN CHINA

Xuefei Ren

polity

First published in 2013 by Polity Press
Reprinted 2014, 2015

Polity Press
65 Bridge Street
Cambridge CB2 1UR, UK

Polity Press
350 Main Street
Malden, MA 02148, USA

ISBN-13: 978-0-7456-5358-7
ISBN-13: 978-0-7456-5359-4(pb)

A catalogue record for this book is available from the British Library.

Typeset in 11.5 on 15 pt Adobe Jenson Pro
by Toppan Best-set Premedia Limited
Printed in the USA by Edwards Brothers Malloy

The publisher has used its best endeavours to ensure that the URLs for external websites referred to in this book are correct and active at the time of going to press. However, the publisher has no responsibility for the websites and can make no guarantee that a site will remain live or that the content is or will remain appropriate.

Every effort has been made to trace all copyright holders, but if any have been inadvertently overlooked the publisher will be pleased to include any necessary credits in any subsequent reprint or edition.

For further information on Polity, visit our website: www.politybooks.com

For the migrant workers in China

Contents

Figures and Tables ——————————————

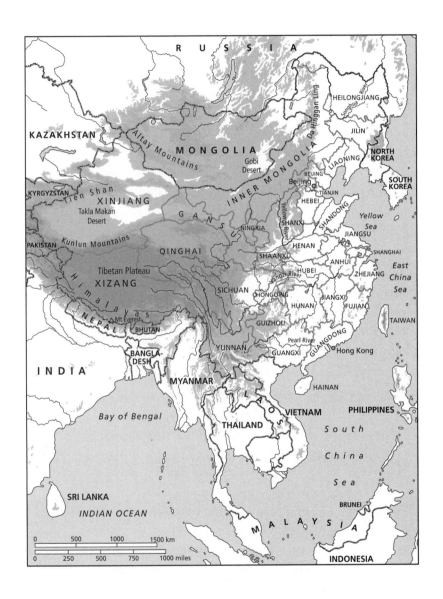

Chronology

March 1959	Tibetan Uprising in Lhasa; Dalai Lama flees to India
1959–61	Three Hard Years, widespread famine with tens of millions of deaths
1960	Sino–Soviet split
1962	Sino–Indian War
October 1964	First PRC atomic bomb detonation
1966–76	Great Proletarian Cultural Revolution; Mao reasserts power
February 1972	President Richard Nixon visits China; "Shanghai Communiqué" pledges to normalize US–China relations
September 1976	Death of Mao Zedong
October 1976	Ultra-Leftist Gang of Four arrested and sentenced
December 1978	Deng Xiaoping assumes power; launches Four Modernizations and economic reforms
1978	One-Child family-planning policy introduced
1979	US and China establish formal diplomatic ties; Deng Xiaoping visits Washington
1979	PRC invades Vietnam
1982	Census reports PRC population at more than 1 billion
December 1984	Margaret Thatcher co-signs Sino-British Joint Declaration agreeing to return Hong Kong to China in 1997
1989	Tiananmen Square protests culminate in June 4 military crackdown
1992	Deng Xiaoping's Southern Inspection Tour re-energizes economic reforms
1993–2002	Jiang Zemin is president of PRC, continues economic growth agenda

November 2001   WTO accepts China as member

August 2002   World Summit on Sustainable Development held in Johannesburg; PRC ratifies 1997 Kyoto Protocol to the United Nations Framework Convention on Climate Change

2003–2012   Hu Jintao is president of PRC

2002–3   SARS outbreak concentrated in PRC and Hong Kong

2006   PRC supplants US as largest CO_2 emitter

August 2008   Summer Olympic Games in Beijing

2010   Shanghai World Exposition

2011   50 percent of the national population live in urban areas

2012   Xi Jinping is president of PRC

Preface

China was historically an agrarian society with the majority of its population engaged in farming and living in rural areas, and this configuration continued until the last quarter of the twentieth century. When the People's Republic of China (PRC) was established in 1949, only 10 percent of the national population lived in cities and, at the dawn of the market reform in 1978, the figure was still less than 20 percent. However, the country has aggressively urbanized since, adding more than 400 new cities and hundreds of millions of urban residents over the last three decades. In 2010, according to the National Bureau of Statistics, about 50 percent of the national population lived in urban areas, 129 Chinese cities had over 1 million residents, and another 110 cities had a population of between half a million and a million. These shifting demographic trends are certainly striking, but the urgency to study Chinese urbanization comes from a different source, that is, the deeper transformation of Chinese society, as manifested in the changing governing institutions, the redistribution of wealth, and the remaking of citizen rights. This book sets out to understand how China has urbanized over a short period of time and what an urbanized China means for its citizens and for the rest of the world.

Before the market reform, China was a two-class society with its population divided into the urban and rural sectors. This configuration was made possible by the enforcement of the *hukou* system, which basically locked each Chinese citizen into a single locality and restricted population movement. In the socialist years, the rural sector was organized around People's Communes, and the urban sector was governed through work units. The rural population was squeezed and exploited to support various industrialization and modernization projects, and the urban population was provided welfare benefits by the state through work units and was better protected from major calamities, such as the Great Famine (1958–61) which caused at least 15 million deaths, mostly in the countryside. This two-class society began to change in the 1980s, as the countryside went through rapid industrialization, and, over the last two decades, the former socialist governing institutions in both the rural and urban sectors have fallen apart or been transformed. The People's Communes were abandoned, work units faded away with reforms of state-owned enterprises, and the *hukou* system has also been reformed in order to allow people to move around and to stimulate the economy. Moreover, major decision-making power has shifted from central ministries to territorial authorities at different scales, especially at the city level. City governments have become powerful players in promoting economic growth and engineering social change.

Urbanization in China has also changed the distribution of wealth and benefits and produced new patterns of inequality. The emergence of the first generation of Chinese billionaires and Fortune 500 companies is accompanied by the swelling ranks of people under the Minimum Living Standard Program – the working poor, the laid-off and unemployed, and impoverished peasants. The 2010 census also recorded 221 million migrants, and most of them have followed the rural-to-urban route. While working and living in the city, rural migrants do not have the same entitlements as their urban counterparts, and this disparity is especially felt by the second-generation migrants who grew up in cities, have no experience in farming, and see themselves as urbanites. In recent years, the sharp inequality has triggered widespread protests, with peasants contesting their land being taken away, middle-class homeowners protesting encroachments on their rights, and workers mobilizing for better wages and treatment. Thus, the new Chinese city has become a strategic site where citizen rights are being reformulated.

A critical analysis of China's urban transition can also bring insights to a number of broader issues, such as the Chinese economy, globalization, and urban theory. First of all, studying China's cities can help us better understand the origin of the Chinese economic miracle. China's economic ascent and its urbanization are closely intertwined, and to understand the economic miracle, one needs to recognize the critical role played by its cities in these processes. Chinese cities, especially the large ones, are the engines driving economic growth in the market-reform era. This is not an arbitrary circumstance, but rather the result of particular policy choices made by the country's top leadership. In the 1990s, the central government began to position large cities at the frontier of economic development by selectively allocating resources and favorable policies to these localities, often at the expense of smaller places and the countryside. The urban bias in policymaking has reshaped the growth trajectory of the Chinese economy since the early 1990s – from rural-centered to urban-centered – and resulted in uneven patterns of development.

China's urban transition also offers a vantage point for understanding the interconnectivity of the global economy. China's urbanization did not happen in a vacuum, but was accompanied by close interaction with the larger world economy. From the sleek skyscrapers in Shanghai to the state-of-the-art Olympics facilities in Beijing and iPhone factories in Shenzhen and Zhengzhou, Chinese cities are remade by transnational flows of capital, information, and expertise. The transformation of the urban economy, communities, and landscape tells a larger story of globalization.

The unprecedented urban growth in China also presents an intriguing case with which to reflect on urban theory developed in the context of Western urbanization. Different from London, New York, Chicago, or Detroit, Chinese cities, and also many other cities in the global South, did not experience high Fordism and the post-Fordist transition, which constitute the basis for major theorizations on urban governance in the West. Although contemporary Chinese cities exhibit similar tendencies of entrepreneurialism and neoliberalization, the causes often have to be sought in developments other than deindustrialization and urban decay, which are not happening or at least have not happened yet in China. A thorough understanding of China's urban transition can open exciting paths for developing new urban theory and vocabularies.

The field of urban China studies has flourished with an extraordinary scholarly output from several disciplines. The main subjects of debate in the field include land and housing reforms, central–local relations, entrepreneurial governance, transformation in the built environment, and rising inequalities. The predominant analytical framework is the institutional approach, which seeks to understand China's urban transition from the perspective of market and state institutions, and the interactions between the two. After more than two decades of research endeavors, we now have a very good picture of the social-spatial restructuring of Chinese cities.

While major progress has been made, there are still a number of glaring gaps to be addressed with continued research. First of all, we still do not know much about the socio-spatial transformation happening in medium and small-sized cities. Most studies so far have focused on the largest cities, such as Beijing, Shanghai, Guangzhou, Chongqing, and Shenzhen. Although there are a moderate number of studies on a handful of second-tier cities, such as Shenyang, Dalian, Xi'an, Kunming, and Wuhan, little is known about the rest of the 600-plus Chinese cities. Readers may find an over-representation of large cities in the case studies in this book, which reflects the current development of the field. During my literature research in both Chinese and English publications, I found that a vast majority of the scholarship focuses on about 10 to 15 of China's largest cities. Whenever possible, I included examples from smaller cities, towns, and villages to show regional diversities and variations. The bias toward the largest cities is not unique to urban China studies, but can be observed in the whole field of global urban studies. So much has been written about the top-tier global cities such as New York, London, Paris, Chicago, and Los Angeles, but relatively little is known about smaller places that are off the radar of urban researchers. In China, small and medium-sized cities are growing even faster than large cities and they provide new frontiers for future research.

Moreover, although certain topics have been thoroughly examined, such as land and housing reforms, other topics have been largely left out, such as gender and the city, ethnic relations in the city, cultural industries, media and the city, the urban food system, and the particularly pressing issue of urban environmental policies and climate change. As these topics get more research attention, we will gain a much fuller picture of the Chinese city.

Lastly, although urban China studies has made significant progress in documenting empirical developments, the field has not made equal progress in reflecting what the Chinese urban experience tells us about existing urban theory, and what role Chinese urbanization plays in the larger system of global capitalism. In the field's current state of development, scholars often borrow theoretical tools and concepts from the West, and compare similarities and differences between the Chinese city and the Western city. This is a first step for advancing comparative urban studies, but the necessary next step is to reflect critically on what Chinese urbanization entails and what it can tell us about the larger world-historical juncture at which we are living. As the frontier of urbanization has unmistakably shifted to Asia, we need new theoretical tools and vocabularies to study this urban process, instead of working the other way around – that is, using urbanization in Asia to prove, reject, or revise Western urban theory.

The motivation for writing this book comes from my own experience of teaching about urban China. For use in my courses, I could not find a single sole-authored book that could give a comprehensive treatment of the Chinese urban condition and engage both specialists and non-specialists. So far, the majority of the scholarly output on Chinese cities has been in the format of specialized journal articles, together with a few research monographs and edited volumes. Most of these publications engage exclusively with specialists and require substantial knowledge on the part of readers in order to follow the debates and exchanges. Moreover, as often pointed out, many publications on Chinese cities are overly empirical, and they become outdated only two to three years after publication. With these shortcomings in mind, this book aims to provide a comprehensive yet critical analysis of Chinese urbanization in an accessible manner.

Drawing upon both the secondary literature and some of my own work, this book examines the past trajectories, present conditions, and future prospects of Chinese cities by investigating five interrelated topics – governance, landscape, migration, inequality, and the cultural economy. Chapter 1 introduces the debate on the rise of China, urban demographic shifts, and the historical evolution of China's urban system. Chapter 2 examines the changing governing structures and institutions, such as the Communist Party, *danwei*, *hukou*, community organizations, governments at different levels, and non-state actors. It also discusses in depth land and housing reforms, infrastructure financing, and the governance of mega-urban regions. This chapter lays a foundation for better understanding other topics in the book and, after chapter 2, readers can skip to any other chapters of interest. Chapter 3 examines landscape changes, discussing a variety of settlement types found both at the center and on the periphery of cities. Chapter 4 examines migration, with particular attention paid to the formation of ViCs (Villages-in-the-City, or migrant enclaves), the factory labor regime, labor protests, and state responses. Chapter 5 examines new patterns of social and spatial inequality and highlights the role of urban renewal in producing wealth and poverty. Chapter 6 introduces the cultural industries, with examples of consumption, nightlife, and art districts. It shows how the urban cultural economy brings both freedom and disempowerment, and how cultural industries have given rise to new forms of state control and intervention. The central theme running through all chapters of the book is the changing citizenship entailed in the urban process, and the various examples demonstrate how the Chinese city has become a strategic ground for reassembling citizen rights.

As the academic life has become more mobile than ever before, I have found myself researching and writing this book in different parts of the world. The first half of the book was written in the spring semester of 2010 at Michigan State University and the following summer in Paris. The second half of the book was written when I was a fellow at the Woodrow Wilson International Center for Scholars in Washington, DC, from September 2011 to May 2012, while simultaneously working on another book project comparing urban governance and citizen rights in China and India. Reading about Indian cities has certainly given me many new perspectives on the Chinese urban condition. One major observation I want to share with the readers of this book is that India, and probably other developing countries as well, have learned many wrong lessons from China, such as setting up Special Economic Zones, advocating massive investments in infrastructure, hosting mega-events, and pushing urban renewal by displacing the poor. Indian cities face many problems and challenges, to be sure, such as housing shortages, poor infrastructure, and high levels of poverty. But following the Chinese model cannot solve these problems. As the Chinese experience shows, massive investment in infrastructure has put local governments in deep debt, and the shining new infrastructure projects often become profit-making machines for private–public partnerships. Hosting mega-events such as the Beijing Olympics has not brought many benefits to the people living in post-event cities, and the Shanghai style of urban renewal has displaced millions of the poor and turned inner-city neighborhoods into exclusive colonies for transnational elites. One of my goals in writing this book is to demonstrate the consequences of Chinese-style urban development and provide a cautionary tale for other cities aspiring to remake themselves into Shanghai. Contrary to the notion of "fast policy transfers," the urban development strategies used in China, as this book shows, have to be unlearned.

I would like to thank the reviewers and my editors at Polity Press for their useful comments and suggestions. My copy-editors Rachel Kamins in Washington, DC, and Helen Gray for Polity Press made all the difference to the text. Shenjing He, Guo Chen, Peilei Fan, Jiang Xu, Yasushi Matsumoto, and Anthony Orum read the whole manuscript and provided useful feedback. My students in the undergraduate seminar "China and Globalization" – from 11 majors across the campus – gave me many ideas on how to make the book accessible to non-specialists. I would like to thank Michigan State University for providing generous research support, and the Woodrow Wilson Center for providing a comfortable yet stimulating environment that made concentrated research and writing not only possible, but also enjoyable.

1 China Urbanized

THE RISE OF CHINA

In 1978, when Deng Xiaoping, the chief architect of China's market reform, returned to leadership after the Cultural Revolution, China was still a backwater – a developing society with a large rural population, an outdated manufacturing sector, and dilapidated housing stock and infrastructure in urban areas. After three decades of market reform, China surpassed France in 2005 and Germany in 2007 to become the third largest economy in the world. And merely three years later, in 2010, China finally overtook the economic powerhouse of Japan, and became the second largest economy next to the United States. From 1978 to 2010, China's GDP grew at 9.99 percent per year on average, which was the highest continuous growth rate among the world's nations (tables 1.1 and 1.2). Its per capita GDP in 2010 was 29,992 RMB (about 4,837 USD), 79 times higher than in 1978 (about 61 USD) when the reform began.[1] Although the benefits of the market reform are unevenly distributed, the continued economic growth has nevertheless lifted hundreds of millions of Chinese out of poverty, and China has finally joined the league of middle-income countries.

China's economic rise has presented an interesting puzzle for social scientists, and scholars have been debating why the country has grown so fast in a relatively short period of time. Two different, but complementary, perspectives can be observed in the debate on China's rise. The first views China's extraordinary growth as part of the worldwide trend of neoliberalization that began in the late 1970s. It relates China's

Table 1.1: China's GDP growth rates, 1978–2010

	GDP GROWTH RATES (IN %)	PER CAPITA GDP (IN RMB)
1978	11.7	381
1979	7.6	419
1980	7.8	463
1981	5.2	492
1982	9.1	528
1983	10.9	583
1984	15.2	695
1985	13.5	858
1986	8.8	963
1987	11.6	1,112
1988	11.3	1,366
1989	4.1	1,519
1990	3.8	1,644
1991	9.2	1,893
1992	14.2	2,311
1993	14.0	2,998
1994	13.1	4,044
1995	10.9	5,046
1996	10	5,846
1997	9.3	6,420
1998	7.8	6,796
1999	7.6	7,159
2000	8.4	7,858
2001	8.3	8,622
2002	9.1	9,398
2003	10.0	10,542
2004	10.1	12,336
2005	11.3	14,185
2006	12.7	16,500
2007	14.2	20,169
2008	9.6	23,708
2009	9.2	25,608
2010	10.3	29,992

Source: China Statistical Yearbook 2011, www.stats.gov.cn

Table 1.2: Shares of GDP and annual growth rates for primary, secondary, and tertiary industries, 1978–2010

	GDP (100 MILLION RMB)	PRIMARY INDUSTRY	SECONDARY INDUSTRY	TERTIARY INDUSTRY
1978	3645.2	1027.5	1745.2	872.5
1990	18667.8	5062.0	7717.4	5888.4
2000	99214.6	14944.7	45555.9	38714.0
2010	401202.0	40533.6	187581.4	173087.0
Annual growth rate				
1978–2010	9.9	4.6	11.4	10.9
1991–2010	10.5	4.0	12.5	10.7
2000–2010	10.5	4.2	11.5	11.2

Note: Data are calculated at current prices.
Source: China Statistical Yearbook 2011

reform measures to marketization and privatization processes taking place in other parts of the world, and sees China's rise as a part, but also a result, of the neoliberal economic restructuring globally (Harvey, 2005). The second view is more attuned to the Chinese historical-local context, and takes China's socialist legacies and post-socialist institutional arrangements as the foundation of the country's spectacular growth (Arrighi, 2007; Huang, 2008).

The first perspective, which explains the rise of China in relation to worldwide neoliberalization, can be further divided into two camps – the promoters and the critics of neoliberalism. According to David Harvey, neoliberalism refers to the political economic proposition that individual freedom and well-being can be best achieved by free markets, free trade, and private property rights, and that the role of the state is to provide institutional frameworks to facilitate free markets and trade and to protect private properties and profit-making activities (Harvey,

2005). Both the promoters and the critics of neoliberalism view China's rise as part of worldwide neoliberalization, but they offer very different explanations of the actual nature of China's adherence to neoliberal doctrines.

The promoters of the free market, such as the World Bank and the International Monetary Fund (IMF), often spread the view that China has been on the fast track of economic growth because the country has adhered to neoliberal policy prescriptions such as privatization, deregulation, and decentralization of fiscal resources and decision-making power from the central to local governments. They believe that with a more open market, a more developed private sector, and a stronger regime of private property rights, eventually the benefits of the market reform will trickle down to the masses. This position, however, is simply not supported by empirical evidence. The economies of a number of Latin American countries, such as Mexico, Argentina, and Jamaica, were devastated after their governments followed structural adjustment policies prescribed by the IMF that included devaluation of currencies, decreases in workers' wages, reduction of social expenditures, privatization of state enterprises, and the opening up of the domestic economy to foreign investment. China's reform measures little resembled these shock therapies. All of these processes happened in China, to a certain degree, but they took place over a longer time period – the reform has continued over a period of more than three decades, and the practice of privatization and deregulation has always been highly selective so that the destructive effects of these market reforms are minimized and delayed.

The critics of neoliberalism question the exploitative growth path China has taken, censuring the current polarization of Chinese society, as evidenced by the widening gaps between the rich and the poor, urban and rural residents, and coastal regions and the hinterland (Harvey, 2005; Arrighi, 2007). Although they do not necessarily think that China's reformers, such as Deng Xiaoping, used the prescriptions of the World Bank or the IMF to guide their actions, they interpret the key reforms China has made, in the sectors of land, housing, and state-owned enterprises, as clear evidence of privatization and deregulation similar to what happened in the West in the 1970s, Latin America in the 1980s and Eastern Europe in the 1990s. For example, David Harvey writes that "the outcome in China has been the construction of a particular kind of market economy that increasingly incorporates neoliberal elements interdigitated with authoritarian centralized control," and he calls this unusual mix of neoliberal elements and authoritarianism "neoliberalism with Chinese characteristics" (2005: 120). He further argues that the market reform in China exemplifies a process of "accumulation by dispossession" – of farmers, urban workers, and migrants – and reconstitutes class power, as evidenced by the sharp increase in income inequality, just like that in the US, the UK, and Latin America.

The critics of neoliberalism are right to point out that China's success story is inseparable from the worldwide neoliberalization that opened up space for China to be integrated into the world economy, and that China has turned from an egalitarian society into a highly polarized one. However, the broad-brush interpretation and categorization of China's reform as an example of generic neoliberalization does not help explain why China has, over such a short period, become the second largest economy in the world, and why other emerging economies such as India, Russia, and Brazil, which also neoliberalized, have not grown at a similar pace.

The second camp of political economic analysis traces China's rise to context- and history-specific conditions and institutional innovations. For example, Giovanni Arrighi identifies two conditions that laid the foundation for what he calls the "Chinese ascent" (Arrighi, 2007). The first is the result of the social legacies of the Chinese revolution and three decades of socialism. Arrighi argues that by the late 1970s China was in a better position to launch its reform than other developing countries such as India, because socialism had delivered high literacy rates, good education, and a long adult life expectancy, and therefore China's labor force was relatively healthy and well educated at the dawn of the reform. China's booming export sector benefited greatly from the country's cheap labor, but Arrighi emphasizes that it was not just the low cost, but also the education and health of the labor reserve that marked a difference from other developing countries and attracted foreign investment.

Second, the early success in rural sectors of Township and Village Enterprise (TVE) initiatives laid firm foundations for the economic take-off later. Deng Xiaoping's reform targeted the agricultural sector first. Between 1978 and 1983, the Household Responsibility System was introduced, under which the decision making power over agricultural surplus was returned to individual rural households. In 1983 – for the first time since 1958, when the *hukou* system[2] was implemented to restrict peasants' mobility – rural residents were given permission to travel outside their villages to seek business opportunities and outlets for their products, and in 1984, farmers were allowed to work in the TVE sectors in nearby towns. TVEs helped to absorb China's huge surplus of labor from the agricultural sector, exert competitive pressure on state-owned enterprises, generate tax revenues for localities, and expand the domestic market (Arrighi, 2007). TVEs also led to rapid industrialization and urbanization of the countryside, and no other developing country had similar success in raising productivity and living standards in rural areas. Overall, focusing on local institutional contexts, Arrighi argues that the legacies of socialism and the achievements of TVEs in the 1980s are what prepared the ground for China's economic miracle later on.

Economist Huang Yasheng attributes China's economic take-off to the TVE initiatives in the 1980s as well, rather than conventional mechanisms of growth such as private ownership, property rights, and financial liberalization. The TVE initiatives of the 1980s, according to Huang, encouraged private entrepreneurship and led to decentralization in the following decades (Huang, 2008). However, rather than viewing China's growth as continuous and accelerating after the initial take-off of the rural sector, Huang notices a rupture in the Chinese growth strategy. He observes that beginning in the early 1990s, China reversed many of its highly productive rural experiments with TVEs, and China's policymakers have since favored cities instead of rural areas for investment and allocation of resources. Shanghai – China's largest commercial city – best illustrates this urban-biased growth model, according to Huang. During the second half of the 1980s, Shanghai's leaders gradually came to dominate national politics by taking top positions in the central government, and since then the central government has initiated many policies favorable to economic development in Shanghai, such as establishing Pudong New District in 1992, the first district of its kind, designed to jump-start a financial center. The Shanghai city government restricted the development of small-scale, entrepreneurial, and rural businesses, and favored instead foreign companies and large enterprises with strong government connections. Contrary to the common praise and admiration for Shanghai, in Huang's account Shanghai is one of the least entrepreneurial cities in the country. Huang argues that the Shanghai model of growth is expensive and leads to sharp social inequality. For example, relative to the national mean, Shanghai's GDP increased massively in the 1990s, but the average household income did not change much. Also, since 2000, during a period of double-digit GDP growth, the poorest population segment in Shanghai has seen its income further decrease. In Huang's narrative of China's ascent, there are two Chinas – the entrepreneurial, market-driven rural China, and the state-led urban China. In the 1980s, rural China gained the upper hand, but in the 1990s, the situation was reversed and Chinese development became more urban-driven.

The two explanations introduced above – one from the perspective of neoliberalization and the other focusing on local institutional arrangements – complement one another, and together they provide a fuller account of the rise of China. It is crucial to recognize the local historical and institutional context in which the transformation from a planned to a market economy took place, but it is also important to keep in mind that China's reform measures would not have been as effective as they were without the larger trends of neoliberal economic restructuring, which opened up space for China to integrate itself into the world economy. Moreover, as Huang Yasheng correctly observes, there was an "urban" turn in the early 1990s in state development policies, evidenced by the massive investment in urban regions, strong intervention by local governments in the micro-management of economic affairs, and tax policies favoring foreign and state-owned enterprises while discriminating against domestic, private, and rural entrepreneurship. In short, China's economic boom since 1990 is an urban boom, and the Chinese miracle is made in its largest urban regions.

THE URBAN TRANSITION

China is the most populous country in the world, and it is no easy task to gather accurate statistics on how many people currently live in the country and how the population is geographically distributed. Beginning in 1953, the government has been conducting a population census about once every ten years – in 1953, 1964, 1982, 1990, 2000, and 2010 – except during the period of the Cultural Revolution. The most recent census, the Sixth National Population Census, was carried out in 2010 and it required more than 1 million census workers to complete.

The past six censuses have documented China's urbanization levels – that is, the percentage of "urban population" in the national total – during the second half of the twentieth century, but demographers and geographers have long pointed out that the criteria used to define the "urban population" vary from census to census; for example, no criteria have been used twice in a row without change (Zhou and Ma, 2003). In the first census in 1953, "urban population" included the total population residing within the administrative boundaries of cities (*shi*) and towns (*zhen*), but in the next census in 1964, only the non-agricultural population residing within the jurisdictions of cities and towns was counted as "urban." The change can be explained by the state effort in the late 1950s and early 1960s to restrict urban population growth so that the state did not have to take care of the social welfare needs of migrants coming from the countryside to live in cities. In the 1990 and 2000 censuses, the criteria used to define the "urban population" became more elaborate – for instance, dividing cities into those with districts and those without, taking account of the population density of places, and starting to count migrants who have lived in cities and towns for more than six months as part of the "urban population." Also, for the first time in the 2000 census, places with a population of more than 3,000 were considered "urban" – no population benchmarks were previously used to define "urban." But many villages with advanced economic development were also counted as "urban" in the census even if their population did not meet the 3,000 benchmark (Zhou and Ma, 2003). In short, the criteria for defining what is "urban" and who counts in the "urban population" have been inconsistent from census to census, and this should be kept in mind when we use census data to discuss China's urban transition.

The 2010 census delivered some alarming, but not completely unexpected, results. Due to the continuing One-Child policy, fertility rates remain at a very low level and China's population growth has definitely slowed down.[3] The total population in 2010 was 1.37 billion, increasing by 5.84 percentage points from 2000, and the annual increase between 2000 and 2010 was only 0.57 percent. The average Chinese household size in 2010 was 3.1 persons, declining from 3.44 persons in 2000. At the same time as the slowing of its growth, China's population continues to move around the country. The 2010 census counted

221 million migrants, defined as people living in a different place from that recorded in their *hukou* registration for six months or longer. The migrant population increased by a staggering 83 percentage points over what it was in 2000.[4]

The continuing economic growth and migration have tipped the balance between the rural and urban populations. China had always had a larger rural population than its urban population in the twentieth century. In the 1982 census, the recorded urban share of the national population was merely 20.6 percent, and, by 1990, it had increased slightly to 26.32 percent. In the 1990s, the urban share of the national population increased by nearly 10 percentage points, to 36.22 percent in 2000 (figure 1.1). The urbanization level of China in 2000 was still much lower than that of other developing countries, such as 59 percent in North Korea, 62 percent in South Africa, 73

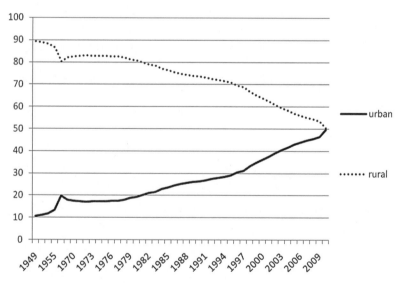

Figure 1.1 Urban population shares in the national population, 1949–2010

Source: China Statistical Yearbooks, 1982–2010.

percent in Russia, 75 percent in Cuba, and 92 percent in Argentina.[5] But the first decade of the twenty-first century saw the largest growth of urban population – by 13.45 percentage points, compared to the earlier decades. The 2010 census reported that between 2000 and 2010 China's urban population expanded by over 200 million, and currently half of China's population lives in urban areas.

As large cities continue to grow, medium-sized and small cities have boomed too, resulting in a relatively even pattern of city-size distribution. In the 1980s, the National Bureau of Statistics classified cities into five categories according to their population size – super-large cities (more than 2 million), extra-large cities (1–2 million), large cities (0.5–1 million), medium cities (0.2–0.5 million), and small cities (less than 0.2 million). These older classifications have become obsolete with the growth of both the number and the size of cities (tables 1.3 and 1.4). In 1981, there were 18 Chinese cities with a population of over 1 million; by 2009, there were 129 cities with a population of over 1 million, and another 110 cities with a population of between 0.5

Table 1.3: Number of cities in different size categories, 1995–2009

	>2 MILLION	1–2 MILLION	0.5–1 MILLION	0.2–0.5 MILLION	<0.2 MILLION
	SUPER-LARGE CITIES	EXTRA-LARGE CITIES	LARGE CITIES	MEDIUM CITIES	SMALL CITIES
1995	10	22	43	192	373
2000	13	27	53	218	352
2005	38	75	108	61	4
2009	42	82	110	51	2

Note: Until 2000, the statistics included both county-level cities and prefecture-level cities. From 2001, the statistics included only prefecture-level cities.
Source: China City Statistical Yearbook, 1996–2010

Table 1.4: 15 Largest cities in 1981 and 2010: a comparison

	1981		2010	
RANK	CITY	POPULATION	CITY	POPULATION
1	Shanghai	6,086,000	Shanghai	15,789,000
2	Beijing	4,665,000	Beijing	11,106,000
3	Tianjin	3,829,000	Guangzhou	9,447,000
4	Shenyang	2,937,000	Shenzhen*	8,114,000
5	Wuhan	2,662,000	Tianjin	7,468,000
6	Guangzhou	2,338,000	Wuhan	7,542,000
7	Harbin	2,094,000	Chongqing	6,690,000
8	Chongqing	1,900,000	Shenyang	4,952,000
9	Nanjing	1,702,000	Dongguan*	4,850,000
10	Xi'an	1,580,000	Chengdu	4,266,000
11	Chengdu	1,376,000	Xi'an	4,178,000
12	Changchun	1,309,000	Guiyang*	3,980,000
13	Taiyuan	1,239,000	Nanjing	3,813,000
14	Dalian	1,208,000	Harbin	3,753,000
15	Lanzhou	1,075,000	Changchun	3,400,000

Note: The data exclude agricultural populations living in urban areas.
* These cities did not appear in the top 15 list in 1981.
Source: 1981 data are from China Statistical Yearbook, 1982. 2010 data are from One World – Nations Online, at http://www.nationsonline.org/oneworld/china_cities.htm, accessed on June 5, 2011.

million and 1 million. Despite the restrictive government measures to curb population growth in super-large cities, the population of Beijing increased by 42 percent, and those of Shanghai and Tianjin grew by 38 and 29 percent between 2000 and 2010.

Population movements follow resources and economic opportunities, which are often found in the largest urban regions. It is no surprise that China's most developed urban regions – the Beijing-Tianjin-

Tangshan urban region, the Yangtze River Delta (Shanghai-Suzhou-Nanjing-Hangzhou), and the Pearl River Delta (Guangzhou-Shenzhen-Dongguan) – have gained the most population, at the expense of the less developed regions in the western interior (figure 1.2). The provinces of Guangdong and Zhejiang grew by 21 percent and 16 percent in population in the period between 1978 and 2000, while western provinces such as Gansu and Sichuan have lost population. Smaller cities grew at an even faster rate than large cities. For example, cities with 0.2–0.5 million people grew by an average of 5.86 percentage points annually between 1978 and 2000, and cities with less than 0.2 million people grew by an average of 5.31 percentage

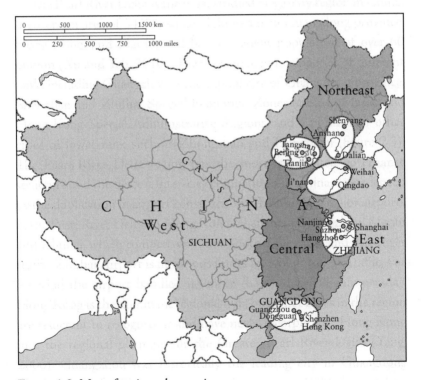

Figure 1.2 Map of major urban regions

points, compared to 4.47 percentage points for cities with over a million people in the same period (Xu and Zhu, 2011). The rapid growth of small cities is a result of the deliberate state policy of controlling the expansion of big cities by developing medium-sized ones and building up small cities since the 1980s.

Urban population growth can be driven by a number of factors, including natural population growth, rural to urban migration, economic developments such as the decline in the farming sector, increasing employment activity in the manufacturing and service sectors, and the pouring of investment into urban areas (Pannell, 2002). In the Chinese case, natural population growth has apparently slowed down due to the One-Child policy, but nevertheless it still contributes significantly to the increase of the urban population because of the large size of the national population. Rural to urban migration has increasingly become the major driving force for urban population growth, spurred by the employment opportunities available in urban areas and the relaxation of the *hukou* system to allow people to move between localities. In addition, a third mechanism is clearly at play for urban population growth: the administrative reclassification of formerly non-urban areas as urban areas, whereby residents living in these places are automatically counted as "urban" even if they still engage in farming activities. Friedmann (2005) estimates that about a fifth of the increase of the urban population in the 1990s is due to administrative reclassification.

There are two types of officially designated urban areas in China – cities (*shi*) and towns (*zhen*). The criteria for classifying places as cities or towns have been significantly relaxed since the 1980s, and many counties have been reclassified as cities. In 1978, there were only 193 cities in the country, but the number increased to 434 in 1988, and to 663 in 2000. Thus, between 1978 and 2000, the country more than tripled its number of officially designated cities. By 2009, China had 654 cities, including prefecture-level cities (i.e., cities with districts), county-level cities (i.e., cities without districts), and the four directly administered municipalities – Beijing, Tianjin, Shanghai, and Chongqing (table 1.5). The addition of new cities has mostly occurred in the more developed coastal regions. In the 1980s and the first half of the 1990s, urban population growth was mostly dependent on the increase in the number of cities, while from the mid-1990s urban growth has been more driven by the expansion of the population size of existing cities (Xu and Zhu, 2011).

HISTORICAL EVOLUTION OF THE URBAN SYSTEM

Recorded urban settlements appeared in the North China Plain as early as the Shang Dynasty (1600–1046 BC), and China's urban system has matured, differentiated, and evolved through the imperial dynasties and into the modern period. Compared to the autonomous urban settlements of the West, Chinese cities historically lacked political autonomy. Three features characterize the Chinese urban system in the imperial period, from the founding of the Qin dynasty in 221 BC to the abdication of the last emperor of the Qing dynasty in 1912.

First, although there were a number of politically powerful cities, China never had a primate system, with one predominant city concentrating the majority of national economic activities and resources. Historically, economic integration advanced around urban centers in several regions, such as the Yellow River Plain and the Yangtze River Delta, which prevented any one of them from becoming nationally dominant (Skinner, 1977). Imperial China also experienced the reshuffling of the capital among major cities, and the fortunes of these capital cities often rose and fell with dynastic transitions. For example, Chang'an (today's Xi'an) flourished during the Han and Tang dynasties; Kaifeng was the imperial capital of the Song dynasty and the major commercial center in the world in the twelfth century; Beijing

Table 1.5: Changes in the number of Chinese cities, 1981–2009

	PREFECTURE-LEVEL CITIES	COUNTY-LEVEL CITIES	TOTAL NUMBER OF CITIES
1981	108	122	230
1982	109	133	242
1983	145	141	286
1984	148	149	297
1985	162	159	321
1986	166	184	350
1987	170	208	378
1988	183	248	431
1989	185	262	447
1990	185	279	464
1991	187	289	476
1992	191	323	514
1993	196	371	567
1994	206	413	619
1995	210	427	637
1996	218	445	663
1997	222	442	664
1998	227	437	664
1999	236	427	663
2000	259	400	659
2001	265	393	658
2002	275	381	656
2003	282	374	656
2004	283	374	657
2005	283	374	657
2006	283	369	652
2007	283	368	651
2008	283	368	651
2009	283	367	650

Note: The data do not include Beijing, Shanghai, Tianjin, and Chongqing. The total number of cities in 2009 is 654, with the four directly administered cities included.

Source: China Statistical Yearbooks, 1982–2000

served as the imperial capital of the Yuan, Ming, and Qing dynasties from the thirteenth to the nineteenth centuries, and was the largest city in the world until 1750. Also, colonial penetration, which is often a major factor in producing a primate city, was limited in the Chinese case; colonial powers never gained complete control over any Chinese city, not even Shanghai (Murphy, 1974; Chen, 1991). Since around the time of the Song dynasty, China has always had a dozen dynamic urban regions, and city size was relatively evenly distributed.

Second, historically, Chinese cities were predominantly administrative centers and their political functions were more significant than their commercial functions in organizing urban social life. At least, this was the case until the boom of market towns in the Ming and Qing periods, as will be explained later in this section. Third, there was no rigid divide between cities and rural areas for most of the country's history, and Chinese cities were closely connected to the countryside and the hinterland through cross-region trade and population movements. It was only in the 1950s, at the beginning of the socialist period, that an urban–rural hierarchy was institutionalized and reinforced. The sharp division between cities and the countryside is a socialist legacy and still significantly shapes Chinese society today.

The urban system before 1949

Unlike in Europe in the Middle Ages, where cities emerged as market towns, Chinese cities throughout most of history were primarily administrative centers and sites for the performance of rituals and ceremonies. Chinese cities in the ancient and imperial periods lacked political autonomy and were dependent on the rural hinterland for resources, and commerce never played a significant role in urban life (Lin, 2007). When Emperor Qin Shi Huang unified China in 221 BC, he made "county" (*xian*) the basic administrative unit, and all administrative functions were concentrated in *xian* capitals, that is, county-seat cities. The county has been the most constant administrative unit of Chinese society for over 2,500 years, and the number of counties and county-seat cities has remained more or less the same until today (Skinner, 1977; Shi, He, and Fan, 2010). In addition to county seats, administrative cities in ancient and imperial China also included prefectural seats, departmental seats, and imperial capitals. These were all political cities with administration as the primary function. They were also consumer cities, with their political and military significance overpowering their economic weight (Liu and Stapleton, 2006).

Max Weber depicts the ancient Chinese city as a political entity without much autonomy, whose citizens lacked an enterprising spirit with regard to urban economic and political affairs (Weber, 1958). According to Weber, Chinese cities never developed a powerful guild system comparable to that of the West during the Middle Ages, and this lack of urban autonomy partially explains the late development in China of legal foundations, modern capitalist organizations, and industries. But works by historians show that Chinese cities in the ancient and imperial periods were not completely buried under administration and bureaucracy. In a study on Hankow in the nineteenth century, Rowe (1992) argues that a distinctive urban consciousness, and a "public sphere," clearly developed within the merchants' communities and neighborhoods in this vibrant commercial town on the Yangtze River.

Overall, however, compared to cities in the West, the lack of development of autonomous commercial cities in the history of China is apparent, and it has to do with the way in which trade and commerce were organized. Confucian doctrine discriminated against commerce, and society was ordered around a hierarchy descending from scholars (*shi*), to farmers (*nong*), to artisans (*gong*), to merchants (*shang*). Although merchants often intermarried with families of government bureaucrats and sent their sons into the bureaucracy, they were never an independent force in cities (Whyte and Parish, 1984). Cities relied on tribute from other regions and did not need to develop trade and commerce on their own in order to survive (Chang, 1977).

The distinction between cities and the countryside was neither clear nor institutionalized throughout most periods of Chinese history. Urban settlements were often surrounded by walls, but the walls were mostly for security and defense purposes and not for separating city-dwellers from rural residents. The vast majority of city-dwellers in ancient and imperial China were peasants who would go out daily through the gates to work in the fields. In urban settlements, during the Qin and Han periods (221 BC to AD 220), the majority of the city population consisted of peasants, followed by government bureaucrats, their families and employees, and a small percentage of residents engaged in crafts, commerce, and trade (Chang, 1977). Writing about the history of Nanking between 1350 and 1400, Mote (1977) argues that the sharp distinctions between rural and urban areas that characterized early modern Europe never existed in late imperial China, and he notes an "organic unity" of urban and rural living that was not seen in the West.

With the growth of the population, commerce expanded and the government gradually withdrew from regulation of commercial affairs. Beginning in the Tang period (618–907), there was a secular trend of retrenchment of government functions and deregulation of commerce and trade. In the Song period (960–1279), many small market towns emerged, and they contrasted sharply with administrative cities. The cities that grew the most were regional economic centers, and it was outside the gates of these cities where markets expanded. Skinner (1977) conceptualizes imperial China as a conglomeration of eight macro-regions, each with a hierarchy of central places surrounding a regional core.[6] Core cities were connected to towns and villages within the same macro-region through economic and political relationships. A well-integrated macro-region urban system may have been achieved during the Tang period around the capital city Chang'an, and during the Song period around the capital city Kaifeng. But until the nineteenth century, because of the limited transportation infrastructure, economic and administrative transactions across macro-regions were too weak to bind the urban systems in each macro-region into an integrated empire-wide urban system.

Due to uneven levels of economic development and political power, urbanization rates varied across regions. North China and the Lower Yangtze area had more advanced urban systems than other regions. North China experienced rapid urban development between the eighth and the thirteenth century, and this was marked by the rise of Kaifeng as the largest city in the region and the center of transport and economic transactions. As a commercial center at the intersection of four major canals, Kaifeng reached its peak in the eleventh century with a population of around 1 to 1.5 million, living both within and outside the three layers of city walls. The vibrant urban life of Kaifeng is vividly captured in the scroll painting by Zhang Zeduan, *Scenes along the River during Qingming Festival* – the most famous painting in Chinese art history, currently in the collection of the Beijing Palace Museum. The population of the central China region reached 33 million in the thirteenth century, but with the invasion of the Mongols, transport was disrupted, the Kaifeng market was destroyed, and most cities in the region declined altogether (Skinner, 1977). Large urban centers also emerged in the lower Yangtze region with the rise of Yangchow (spelled today as Yangzhou), Soochow (Suzhou), and Hangchow (Hangzhou).

Regional integration proceeded with the advance of means of transportation and the opening of China to foreign trade after the two Opium Wars (1839–42 and 1856–60). The urban system in the Qing dynasty (1644–1912) was marked by the development of canal cities, treaty port cities, and railway cities. First, in the Qing dynasty, existing cities along the Grand Canal further developed and new ones emerged too. With a total length of 1,776 kilometers, the Grand Canal begins in Beijing, goes through Hebei, Shandong, Jiangsu, and Zhejiang provinces, and ends in Hangzhou. The major canal cities include Hangzhou, Suzhou, Yangzhou, Tianjin, Dezhou, Linqing, Ji'ning, Huai'an, and Tongzhou. The canal facilitated transportation of goods and resources across the regions, and the cities along the route formed a transregional network independent of the traditional urban system (Liu and Stapleton, 2006). In the wake of its military defeat, the Qing dynasty signed the Treaty of Nanjing in 1842 with the British, which gave birth to the second new type of city – treaty ports. Treaty ports were places that were forced to open to foreign trade through unequal treaties signed between China and Western imperial powers. The first treaty ports in China, established with the Treaty of Nanjing, were Shanghai, Canton (Guangzhou), Ningbo, Foochow (Fuzhou), and Amoy (Xiamen). Through the early twentieth century, more than 80 treaty-port cities appeared across the country (Feuerwerker, 1983). Many of the treaty ports were extraterritorial entities where foreign powers were given authority to build "concessions" that were not subject to the Chinese legal and court systems. The leading example of such cities is Shanghai, which surpassed Beijing as the largest city in China in the 1930s. As treaty ports became major urban centers, they reshaped the traditional urban system revolving around administrative cities. And soon, with the construction of national railway networks in the early twentieth century, there appeared railway cities functioning as regional transportation nodes, such as Hankou (on the Beijing–Hankou railway) and Harbin (on the Sino–Russian railway).

To summarize, there were several distinctive types of Chinese cities before 1949, including administrative cities, market towns, canal cities, treaty ports, and railway cities. The traditional Chinese urban system was centered around administrative cities before the middle imperial period – until around the time of the Song dynasty; after that, with population growth and expansion of trade, cities with strong commercial functions flourished and an empire-wide urban system gradually developed. Sharp distinctions between urban and rural areas did not exist. Even in the Republican period, which witnessed the emergence of Western-influenced cities such as Shanghai, historians note that these modern Chinese cities were very much shaped by the rural culture brought by migrants from the countryside, who tried to establish familiar patterns of life in their new urban setting (Lu, 1999; Liu and Stapleton, 2006).

Industrialization without urbanization: 1949–1978

The traditional Chinese urban system that had evolved through the dynasties and the Republican era was fundamentally altered during the communist rule beginning in 1949. China in 1949 was a predominantly agrarian society with only 10 percent of its population living in cities. The urban system inherited by the communist regime had only a few large cities, and the majority of the urban population was concentrated in these cities. Geographer George Lin argues that the communist regime reorganized the pre-existing traditional Chinese urban system in two ways. First, large cities enjoyed significant expansion by assuming both economic and political functions – economically, they were the places with the most advanced industrial infrastructure, and politically, these cities also corresponded with provincial capitals. Second, the formerly underdeveloped northeast, central, and western regions received targeted investment and experienced rapid urban population growth, while cities on the east coast experienced decline and neglect during the socialist years (Lin, 2002). This dispersed pattern of urban growth created by channeling resources and investment from the coastal region to the interior was driven by the government's commitment to national development as well as concerns over national security during the Cold War period. The egalitarian principles of socialism aimed to eliminate "Three Differences" – between industry and agriculture, between cities and the countryside, and between mental and manual labor. But, ironically, some of these differences were amplified, and even ossified, as a result of policy choices made under socialism.

Mao Zedong's communist revolution succeeded first in rural areas with the mobilization of peasants, and there was a clear anti-urban bias in national policymaking during the socialist period. Mao himself disliked large cities, and he was known to remark that "it's no good if cities are too big" (Naughton, 1995). Under the influence of Soviet urban-planning ideology, cities were seen as sites for industrial production rather than for consumption and developing service industries. National leaders believed that consumption and investment in urban infrastructure such as housing and transportation were nonproductive and therefore should be kept to the minimum possible level. To avoid the costs of urbanization, the size of cities and the urban population were strictly controlled during the socialist years. The urban population increased by only 2.3 percent annually in the 1960s and 1970s, and it never exceeded 20 percent of the national population. Kirkby (1985) notes that the purpose of restricting urban consumption under socialism was to enhance the role of cities as industrial production centers, and that China's urbanization was shaped by the industrialization imperative.

The geographic distribution of cities during the socialist period closely followed the national priorities of industrial development (Lin, 2002). During the First Five-Year Plan period (1953–7), the central government announced a list of 156 key construction projects for industrialization, which led to the expansion of existing cities and the creation of new ones.[7] Both the number of cities and the size of the urban population saw an increase in this period. State investment was poured into cities in the northeast in the 1950s, such as Harbin, Changchun, and Shenyang. In the 1960s, concerned with national security and the threat of nuclear attacks from the United States, the central government initiated the Third Front project, to disperse industrial facilities from the east coast and northeast to the mountainous regions in the southwest. The Third Front project was tremendously costly, and not very effective: most of the country's industrial facilities remained concentrated in large cities on the east coast throughout the socialist period. Beginning with the Cultural Revolution in the mid-1960s, the growth of cities stagnated, and between 1965 and 1978, more than 17 million city youths were sent to the countryside to be "re-educated" by peasants. By the late 1970s, China stood out among developing countries for its disinvestment in cities and slow pace of urbanization.

Not only did the socialist government disinvest from and neglect cities, but it extracted their resources to subsidize national development (Naughton, 1995). In the 1960s and 1970s, the government both restricted the growth of cities and channeled resources away from large coastal cities to other regions in the country. Naughton (1995) argues that despite the communist government's anti-urban biases, it had to rely on cities to collect financial resources in order to plan and run the national economy. Shanghai is an example. The city was the most advanced industrial center in the country, but had to turn most of its revenues over to the central government to be reinvested in other regions. There was little investment in Shanghai's housing and infrastructure in the socialist decades, so that by the late 1970s, the city had acquired a museum-like look, with its dilapidated neoclassical and art deco buildings from the colonial era.

The policy choice of "industrialization without urbanization" not only suppressed urban consumption, but also destroyed the formerly diversified rural economy and produced a sharp distinction between cities and the countryside. Rural China before socialism had thriving craft industries and commerce, but by the mid-1960s, due to collectivization, the rural economy had become overwhelmingly concentrated in agricultural production (Fei, 1986). As commerce, crafts, and service industries were discouraged, more than 90 percent of the rural population was engaged in farming only, which was unprecedented in the country's history. Cities specialized in manufacturing and rural areas specialized in agricultural production. The distinction between urban and rural areas had never before been as sharp as it became in the socialist years. In spite of the lack of investment in cities, urban residents at least enjoyed the benefits of state-provided housing, schools, hospitals, and other social welfare provisions, which were not available to rural residents, and this triggered a rapid migration from the country-side to cities in the 1950s. Unable to support the influx of rural migrants, in 1958 China introduced the *hukou* system, dividing the national population into urban and rural segments and restricting population movement between cities and the countryside. Thus, the urban–rural divide in Chinese society was aggravated by the state priorities of industrialization and the suppression of urbanization, and later was institutionalized with the *hukou* regime.

THE URBAN BOOM: 1980S–PRESENT

Socialist urban policies were reversed in the 1980s, and the urban system was reorganized by the new priorities of the market reform. In the decade of the 1980s, urbanization took the form of rural industrialization through TVEs, a process often referred to as "urbanization from below" (Ma and Cui, 2002). Beginning in the 1990s, the center of urbanization shifted back to cities, with large-scale capital investments flowing into urban areas. This is described as a shift from "rural-based urbanization" to "city-centered urbanization" (Lin, 2002).

Urbanization of the countryside: the 1980s

Before the reform, manufacturing and commercial activities in villages and towns were underdeveloped, and the economic activity of rural localities was largely restricted to farming. The Household Responsibility System was introduced in the late 1970s, and it replaced the collective farming practices under the previous system of People's Communes by giving farmers greater incentive to increase production. By 1984, People's Communes had been abolished completely. The enhanced agricultural productivity released a large amount of surplus labor and provided impetus for TVEs. Most TVEs interacted closely with local governments of towns and villages, and it was common for government officials to serve as managers and executives in these rural enterprises. The political careers of local officials largely depended on the economic performance of TVEs under their supervision, which provided extra incentive for local officials to be involved in the management and business activities of TVEs. The close relationship between local government and business is described as "local state corporatism" (Oi, 1992, 1999). The TVEs under the control of local governments could retain a significant portion of their profit after they had satisfied the fiscal responsibilities agreed upon between them and their superior administrative agencies. Local officials could benefit from various types of perks from the enterprises under their control, while residents also enjoyed higher income, increased job opportunities, and expanded social programs as TVEs thrived (Ma and Cui, 2002).

TVEs were the major mechanism of urbanization in the countryside in the 1980s, and there have been a number of distinctive models of TVE development and rural urbanization, reflecting the variations in the socio-economic conditions and institutional arrangements from region to region. The most studied are the Guangdong, Wenzhou, and Sunan models. In Guangdong, TVEs of mixed ownership engaged in subcontracted manufacturing and relied on investment coming in mostly from Hong Kong through family and kinship ties (Leung, 1996). In Wenzhou of Zhejiang province, TVEs were mostly privately owned and tended to specialize in certain products. In southern Jiangsu province (the Sunan region), TVEs were typically collectively owned and managed by town and village governments. In spite of the variations, what was common in TVE-led industrialization was active local leadership taking advantage of both regulatory changes such as fiscal decentralization and investment capital from domestic and overseas sources.

The making of a button town

The tens of thousands of villages and towns in China experimented with various strategies to urbanize and industrialize, such as setting up small special economic zones and industrial parks, promoting real-estate development to attract rural peasants to live in nearby towns, and specializing in single products. Ma and Cui (2002) conducted a series of case studies on the urbanization of rural towns in the mid-1990s. Below is the story of Qiaotou town in Zhejiang province, which transformed itself from an impoverished agricultural village into the largest manufacturing and wholesale center for buttons in Asia.

Qiaotou was an isolated town with a population of 64,000 in 1994, located in the hills of southern Zhejiang, about 40 km from Wenzhou. Its growth had nothing to do with its location or local resources. Before the reform, the town was known for its traveling cotton fluffers (*tan mianhua de*). Cotton quilts and coats were commonly used by people throughout China to keep warm in winter, and lumps would form in the cotton with use. Cotton fluffers traveled the country and made a modest living by offering to loosen the lumps in cotton quilts and coats. Qiaotou's cotton fluffers saw business potential in manufacturing and marketing buttons in their travels. Since manufacturing buttons required little skill, technology, or capital, small family workshops engaged in this business soon emerged in Qiaotou, and, in the meantime, traveling merchants from Qiaotou bought buttons made elsewhere and brought them back to their town for wholesale. The town's button business grew rapidly. According to Ma and Cui (2002), by the mid-1990s, it had become the largest wholesale center for buttons in Asia, accounting for 80 percent of the country's total button trade. The town government built 2,000 button stalls where more than 1,800 types of buttons were traded, 80 percent of which were produced locally. The town government collected rent income by leasing the stalls to sellers and also taxes from small enterprises making and trading buttons. The clustering of button makers, sellers, and sales agents led to the growth of a range of tertiary services in the town, such as restaurants, hotels, grocery stores, and transportation services. As Ma and Cui (2002) note, Qiaotou is a classic example of place-based specialization and agglomeration of small-scale production. In the same area around Wenzhou, there are many other towns specializing in a single product, such as Liushi (electronic goods and small household hardware), Yishan (synthetic fabrics), Jinxiang (trademark tags and pin buttons), Xiaojiang (woven plastic bags), and Xianjiang (plastic sandals). But single-product specialization is only one of the many paths taken in the urbanization and industrialization of the Chinese countryside.

City-centered urbanization: 1990s–present

The focus of development shifted from rural to urban areas in the late 1980s and early 1990s, with the designation of dozens of cities on the east coast as special economic areas and development zones. First, the central government selected four cities in Guangdong and Fujian provinces – Shenzhen, Zhuhai, Shantou, and Xiamen – as Special Economic Zones (SEZs), where favorable policies on land leasing, taxation, and labor regulations were introduced to attract investment from overseas Chinese diasporas in Hong Kong, Taiwan, and Southeast Asia. As the SEZ experiment in the south became an immediate success, in 1984 the central government designated another 14 coastal cities as "Open Cities," for example, Dalian, Qinhuangdao, and Tianjin, to attract foreign investment (figure 1.3). In 1988, the entire Hainan province was turned into an SEZ and, in 1991, the central leadership

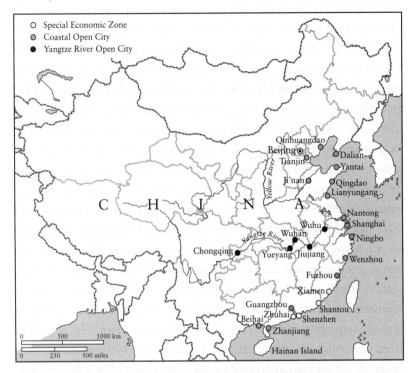

Figure 1.3 Map of Special Economic Zones and other cities with special status

decided to jump-start Shanghai by establishing Pudong New District and developing it into the primary financial center in the country. By the end of the 1990s, SEZs and "development zones" (*kaifaqu*) of various kinds had mushroomed across the country, signaling the shift of policy priorities to urban areas.

The shift from rural to city-centered urbanization is the result of a number of factors, such as China's increased integration into the world economy in the 1990s, fiscal and administrative decentralization, and foreign investment pouring into urban areas. The city-centered urbanization is characterized by decisions to invest in major urban projects by bureaucratic elites from the central and municipal governments. For example, in the late 1980s, the central government was concerned with the slow pace of Shanghai's growth, and the central leadership – composed mostly of former leaders of Shanghai, such as Jiang Zemin and Zhu Rongji – worried that Shanghai would be left behind other cities such as Guangzhou and Shenzhen. In 1991, the central government decided to build Shanghai into China's primary global city and financial center, pouring a large amount of capital into the building of Pudong New District. By pulling resources from other regions and investing massively in infrastructure, the central policy quickly breathed new life into the city and, in the next two decades, Shanghai continued to be a beneficiary of policies and a target of investment. From a dilapidated socialist city with crumbling infrastructure to an international metropolis with sleek skyscrapers and a state-of-the-art public transit system, the transformation of Shanghai after the 1990s is clearly a result of urban-centered development policies.

CONCLUSIONS

This chapter has introduced the major debates on China's economic rise, recent demographic trends of urbanization, and the historical evolution of China's urban system. The main points of the chapter can be summarized as follows. First, China's economic rise has to be explained by both exogenous forces, such as the worldwide process of neoliberalization since the 1970s, and the endogenous factor of local institutional arrangements, such as the TVE initiatives. Second, even accounting for the often inconsistent criteria for defining the "urban population" in Chinese censuses, the urbanization rate has increased rapidly in the post-reform period, with an increasing number of new cities and the expansion of the population of existing cities. Third, the Chinese urban system has evolved over the imperial, republican, socialist, and post-reform periods. Cities in imperial China lacked political autonomy, and trade and commerce did not play a major role in shaping urban social life until the late imperial era. Socialist urban policies were characterized by industrialization without urbanization, dispersion of development across the country, and disinvestment and channeling of resources from large coastal cities to the rest of the country. The rural sector was heavily exploited to support industrialization in the socialist years. In the reform era, urbanization shifted from a rural-centered, *in situ* transformation of the countryside in the 1980s to city-centered urbanization in the 1990s. China's economic rise was jump-started by the TVE initiatives of the 1980s, but relied more on capital accumulation through large-scale urban development after the 1990s.

2 | Governance

Property-related disputes are nothing new in Chinese cities, as urban residents and farmers routinely lose their homes and land to various development projects initiated by local governments and private developers. But a story on land seizures in the city of Chongqing in November 2011 caught my attention, with its unusual twists. In 2011, the national Ministry of Land issued a stop order to a villa-resort project near Chongqing. The developer, China Overseas Holdings Ltd, planned to invest 16 billion RMB in the project, building an 18-hole golf course, a hunting zone, and a 258-room five-star hotel. The project is located in a scenic region, near a lake with 38 peninsulas and islands in a valley, and the local Nanchuan district government wanted it to be an "eco-tourism" demonstration, modeled after resorts in Switzerland. In addition to the development rights, the developer also received 200 hectares from the district government for free.

The focus of contention was the seizure of farmland by the local government and the displacement of farmers who had cultivated the land for generations. The Ministry's order, however, did not stop the project; the developer paid fines of 4.1 million RMB and resumed construction, with support from both the Chongqing city government and the Nanchuan district government, which never signed off on the stop order from the Ministry. The local branch of the Law Enforcement Unit of the Ministry of Land did not enforce the order either. The news reached Beijing and the Ministry sent a special team to investigate the case, and, at the end of the investigation, eight local party officials were "disciplined" and had to resign.

But even the firing of district officials could not put a stop to the project. The construction continued due to the persistence of the district government and the developer, and all farmers were forced to leave their land. The last farmer to hold out, Mr Du, told journalists that the town government and demolition office sent officials from the Education Department who threatened that his children, who were teachers at local schools, would be fired if he did not agree to relocate. So Mr Du finally gave in. The developers offered each farmer 250 RMB (about 40 dollars) to cover transition expenses and a free apartment in a low-rise residential complex squeezed into a small section of the project site. The resettlement housing had not yet been built when farmers' houses were demolished, and some had to live in barns with pigs during the cold winter. When the farmers finally moved into their new apartments, they found the quality of the construction so poor that the roofs and walls were already leaking. To keep the farmers from making claims over land in the future, the local government also changed their *hukou* status from "agricultural" to "non-agricultural."[1]

This story of land seizures raises many questions pertinent for understanding Chinese urban governance today. For example, what is the power dynamic between central ministries and local governments? What is the relationship between central ministries and their local law-enforcement branches? What are the incentives behind local governments' feverish support for developers? In this case, eight officials were fired, but still the local government continued to back the developer. Also, what institutional factors put Chinese citizens in such a disadvantaged position when negotiating with the government and developers in land disputes? And what are the implications of changing farmers' *hukou* status from "agricultural" to "non-agricultural"? This chapter addresses these questions by examining both the formal structures and the informal practices of urban governance among state and non-state actors.

Recent studies suggest that urban governance in China has similar features as in postindustrial cities in the West, such as neoliberalism and urban entrepreneurialism, whereby city governments act like corporations and form alliances with non-state actors to engage in competition with other localities in order to promote urban growth (He and Wu, 2009). While similar neoliberal tendencies can be observed in urban governance practices in China and the West today, it is also necessary to recognize that Chinese cities did not go through the same post-Fordist transition as in the West, which forms the background for theorizations on neoliberalism and entrepreneurialism (Brenner and Theodore, 2002). Instead of the crisis of Fordism, it is the regulatory framework inherited from the socialist era that has presented a problem for meeting the new demands of urbanization and migration in China. Since the 1990s, new forms of entrepreneurial governance have emerged and intense competition for more investment and faster growth among localities has become rampant. The vast socio-economic transformations accompanying the country's opening-up have presented new challenges to China's current governance system, characterized by one-party rule, rigid hierarchy, local entrepreneurialism, and a lack of democratic representation and popular participation in policy-making and politics. After three decades of market reform, China is at a crossroads and in desperate need of building effective institutions to govern its cities and regions in order to deliver growth in a more sustainable and egalitarian manner.

This chapter first examines the formal administrative hierarchy in which cities are embedded and the changing socialist institutions such as *danwei*, *hukou*, and the Chinese Communist Party (CCP). Decentralization of decision-making authority and fiscal resources from the central to local levels is one of the most salient features of the market reform. The chapter examines how decentralization has occurred, how municipal governments have fared in the process – they have fared very well, and often at the expense of other territorial units – and where power lies in the current decentralized governance structure. Focusing on urban regions, the chapter analyzes the changing governance structure in the three sectors of land, housing, and infrastructure. In the final sections, a closer look at urban governance focuses on two specific scales – mega-city regions and communities.

Two major observations can be made about the maze-like, complex Chinese urban-governance system. First, urban governance in today's China is characterized by the territorialization of the state – a process in which power is shifted from central ministries in Beijing to territorial authorities at different scales. Among the different scales, the urban scale – that of cities and city-regions – has gained the most power at the expense of other territorial units, especially rural counties, townships, and villages. Second, "decentralization" should not be understood too literally, as a one-way devolution of power from the center to localities. Instead of viewing the center and localities as engaged in a zero-sum game for power and resources, it is more accurate to describe what is occurring in present-day China as a win–win game – both central and local authorities have strengthened their capacity to govern, and whether power lies at the center or below largely varies according to time periods, policy issues, and the perceived importance of the issues among China's top leadership.

IMPERIAL LEGACIES

China had a distinctive political culture and an elaborate system of bureaucracy in its imperial past. A centralized bureaucratic apparatus was established when Qin Shi Huang unified the country more than

2,000 years ago, and the Chinese system of governance evolved from that time with the rise and fall of dynasties. Political scientist Kenneth Lieberthal (2004) describes China's traditional polity as a blending of both the lofty Confucian ideology emphasizing hierarchy, order, tradition, and harmony and tough Legalist measures advocating material rewards and harsh punishments. Confucian thought was the official ideology for most of the imperial period, and it is characterized by conservatism – looking not to the future but to the past to identify the ideal society; hierarchy – preserving rank orders in both political and social spheres; and moral doctrines – emphasizing correct conduct for social relationships and interactions, which is considered the key to a harmonious society (Lieberthal, 2004). The rulers of China also adhered to Legalism, a school of political philosophy advocated by Han Fei Tzu in the Warring Kingdoms Period (475–221 BC). Legalism assumes that human nature is lazy and evil, and only physical punishments and material rewards can deliver desired results for rulers. Qin Shi Huang adopted Legalism as his guiding political ideology and, during his rule, China saw massive mobilization of labor and the construction of mega projects, such as the Great Wall, major water infrastructure, and the massive Qin tombs with thousands of life-sized terracotta warriors in today's Xi'an, made to protect the emperor after his death. The emperor, called *tianzi*, meaning "the son of heaven," was above the law, regulations, and bureaucracies, and he was supposed to set the moral framework for the entire society through correct conduct of behavior and rituals.

The imperial system has clear legacies in contemporary Chinese forms of governance, such as the concentration of power in strong leaders unbounded by laws and regulations, and the imbalance of power between those strong leaders and institutions (Lieberthal, 2004). Many of the features of imperial Chinese bureaucracy not only survived but were further strengthened by the authoritarian regime of the communist era, and their legacies can still be clearly observed today.

For example, in both government organizations and private enterprises, top leaders are often referred to as *yibashou*, literally meaning "number one leader." The *yibashou* often has absolute power in organizational decision-making and personnel appointments, and employees tend to spend an enormous amount of energy on guessing the preferences of the *yibashou* and trying to please him or her.

Confucian and Legalist ideas can be seen in many spheres of governance today, such as the hierarchical organization of the national administration, the centralization of power in a handful of leaders, the power imbalance between leaders and institutions, and material rewards and punishments for officials from their supervisors in the upper ranks. Like imperial rulers, the communist party-state occasionally still attempts to set the moral framework for the society at large, as for instance in the Party's campaign of "Three Representations," a term coined by then-President Jiang Zemin in 2000 in an attempt to extend party organizations to the private sector and new social groups. Jiang claimed that the CCP should represent advanced socialist production, advanced Chinese culture, and the interests of the people. Such moral campaigns launched by the Party, however, frequently become targets for popular parody. For instance, responding to the vast discontent over the rising inequality, the administration of Hu Jintao and Wen Jiabao invoked Confucian ideals and put forward the slogan of building a "harmonious society" (*hexie shehui*). People often mock this slogan with reference to "river crabs" (*hexie*), a phrase with the same pronunciation as "harmonious" in Chinese. In 2010, artist and provocateur Ai Weiwei hosted a party in his brand-new studio in Shanghai and announced that he would serve river crabs to his guests as the main dish, to protest the order from the municipal government to tear down his studio.[2] *Hexie* has also come to be used as a verb, and government crackdowns on popular protests are often described as protesters being "harmonized" by the government (*bei hexie le*).

FORMAL ADMINISTRATIVE HIERARCHY

China's formal administration system is often described as a matrix of *tiao* and *kuai* (i.e., lines and pieces). *Tiao* refers to the vertical administrative units under the supervision of the State Council in Beijing, such as ministries (e.g., the Ministry of Rail, the Ministry of Housing and Urban-Rural Development), commissions (e.g., the National Development and Reform Commission), institutions (e.g., the Chinese Academy of Social Sciences, Xinhua News Agency), bureaus (e.g., the State Postal Bureau), special offices (e.g., the State Administration of Industry and Commerce), and the Central Bank (i.e., the Bank of China). *Kuai* refers to territorial administrative units such as the governing bodies of provinces (*sheng*), cities (*shi*), counties (*xian*), towns (*zhen*), townships (*xiang*), and villages (*cun*). Currently, China has 31 province-level administrative units, including 22 provinces, 5 autonomous regions, and 4 directly administered municipalities (figure 2.1).

The vertical *tiao* and horizontal *kuai* thus divide the country into a matrix of overlapping authorities. In the socialist era, power lay mostly

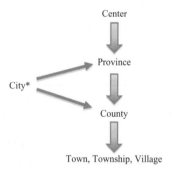

Figure 2.1 China's formal administrative hierarchy
Note: City is a multi-rank administrative unit. There are cities at different levels.

in *tiao* – i.e., the central government and the vertical ministries – and *kuai* (i.e., territorial units) did not have substantial power in managing their own affairs. One of the major changes brought about by market reform is the reversal of the *tiao–kuai* relationship, with territorial authorities gaining more power and access to resources, and central ministries and their branches becoming regulatory bodies that do not directly interfere in local affairs.

Province

The province is a major territorial unit in China's administrative hierarchy. China's provinces vary in size, wealth, economic structures, geography, dialect, and culture. Conventionally, the country is divided into four regions – east, central, west, and northeast. The most developed provinces are found in the eastern region and part of the central region, and the least developed provinces are mostly in the western region. The northeast region has three provinces – Heilongjiang, Jilin, and Liaoning. The region received massive industrial investment during the socialist period but has suffered the most from reforms of state-owned enterprises since the early 1990s. The Second National Economic Census, conducted in 2008, showed that over 50 percent of the industrial units engaged in the secondary and tertiary sectors were in the eastern region of China, and the distribution of the enterprises clearly showed a descending pattern from east to west. There were 3.73 million legally registered units in the eastern region in 2008, accounting for 52.5 percent of the total. The central, west, and northeast regions had 1.41 million, 1.37 million, and 0.59 million legally registered enterprises, respectively, comprising about 20 percent, 19.2 percent, and 8.3 percent of the total.[3] Provinces in the eastern region are more integrated into the world economy than those in other regions of the country.

The GDP of some large Chinese provinces is often bigger than the GDP of other whole countries. For example, in 2010, the GDP of

Guangdong province was greater than that of Switzerland; the GDP of Shanghai, which is a province-level municipality, was greater than that of Finland; and the GDP of Liaoning province, in the industrial rustbelt of the northeast region, was greater than that of Singapore. The GDP of Guangdong in 2010 was 12 times greater than the combined total GDP of the three poorest provinces – Ningxia, Qinghai, and Tibet – indicating the country's uneven regional development.[4] Economic structures also vary greatly from province to province. Shanghai has a high concentration of large-scale high-tech manufacturing facilities such as semi-conductor fabrication plants, while Guangdong is dominated by smaller-scale and privately owned light manufacturers, making clothes, toys, and consumer electronics.

A fundamental goal of the market reform has been to encourage provinces to become more self-reliant and entrepreneurial by experimenting with new policies and approaches to accelerate local economic growth. The relationship between the central government and provinces is largely a cooperative one, but there are cases where provincial officials evade orders from the center that are not top priority and not specific (Lieberthal, 2004). In terms of rank, a province is equal to a ministry in the central government; therefore, ministers cannot issue binding orders for provinces to obey, and when conflicts arise, they have to be negotiated among provincial officials and central ministers (Lieberthal, 2004). This explains the aforementioned land dispute in Chongqing, in which the stop order from the Ministry of Land did not have binding power over the city government, because Chongqing is one of the four province-level municipalities and the mayor of Chongqing has equal rank to the Minister of Land. In provincial and city governments, there are corresponding administrative units that are counterparts of and report to the central ministries, but most central ministries do not directly lead their local counterparts, and the government ministries at the local level often cannot exercise control over local affairs. In the Chongqing land dispute, in response to pressure from the city and district governments, the local branch of the Ministry of Land did not enforce the order from Beijing.

City

The city was officially adopted as an administrative unit in China in the early twentieth century. In 1909, the central government issued the *Regulations for the Local Self-Government of Cities, Towns and Rural Communities*, and, for the first time in China, city governments were recognized as administrative units in their own right (Elvin, 1974). The first modern Chinese city administrations appeared in two Western-influenced treaty ports – Shanghai and Tianjin – in the first decade of the 1900s. The establishment of city administration in Republican China was part of the larger movement of municipalization that had been going on in Europe and other parts of the world since the late eighteenth century. From that time to the mid-nineteenth century, national governments in European countries began to grant legal status to city governments. France established a common law for local communes with the Decree of 1789. England passed the Municipal Corporations Act in 1835 to create a standard for incorporating cities. By the mid-nineteenth century, most other Western European countries, including Germany, Belgium, Denmark, Sweden, and Italy, had enacted their own municipality laws to grant legal status to cities (Saunier, 2008). The British formula of cities being incorporated by the national legislature was soon adopted in North America and other British colonies such as India and Australia. Municipal councils appeared in British-controlled Shanghai as early as 1854 and, in 1905, the first modern Chinese city administration was established in Shanghai under clear Western influence (Saunier, 2008; Elvin, 1974). Power to manage local affairs was transferred from the appointed county magistrates to the elected members of municipal councils. Urban historians point out that new city councils in Republican China did not simply import models of city government from Europe, and neither did they constitute a clear break from older practices of local governance. Writing about the city administration in Shanghai between 1905 and 1914, Elvin (1974) argues that the Shanghai municipal government that emerged after 1905 was largely a hybrid of previously existing indigenous institutions and elites, such as county gentries, gentry-run charitable foundations, and merchants' guilds, which had some knowledge of Western city governments. Inspired by the model of a municipal welfare state, the new city council undertook projects of urban planning, sanitation, and the development of police forces and primary schools. Although elected city councils appeared in many treaty-port cities, the city as an administrative unit was not clearly defined in the Constitution and its legal status remained weak throughout the Republican period.

In the 1950s, the communist government recognized the city as a legal and administrative unit in order to advance its urban-based industrialization policies. The CCP also installed the *hukou* system to clearly demarcate the boundary between cities and countryside. In the administrative hierarchy in today's China, the city is a multi-scalar entity that can be plugged into any of the administrative levels from province to county (Lieberthal, 2004). In addition to the four province-level cities, there are more than 600 cities at the sub-provincial, prefecture, and county levels. City governments at these different levels have different degrees of authority. For example, the mayor of Guangzhou, a sub-provincial city and the capital of Guangdong province, has more power at his disposal than the mayor of Zhongshan, a prefecture-level city in the same province.

District, county, town, township, village

Smaller territorial units below provinces and province-level cities include city districts, counties, towns, townships, and villages. In general, power and authority tend to decrease down the hierarchy from the central to the local, but many of the smaller territorial units, such as district governments, townships, and even village governments, have become increasingly powerful and entrepreneurial, by actively supervising, stimulating, and participating in their local economic affairs, especially through leasing land and attracting business investment. To use the example of the Chongqing land dispute again, the Nanchuan district government played a major role in displacing local farmers, by choosing a private developer and co-investing in the project, offering free land to the developer as an incentive, supporting the developer when the Ministry of Land issued the stop order, and mobilizing subordinate departments to coerce farmers into relocating. As will be discussed later in this chapter, the dependence of local revenues on land-leasing fees and taxes paid by developers explains why local governments are often the most enthusiastic partners in such disruptive projects.

SOCIALIST GOVERNING INSTITUTIONS: THE PARTY, *DANWEI*, AND *HUKOU*

Geographer Fulong Wu describes *danwei, hukou,* and the party as the three pillars of socialist urban governance (Wu, 2002). Together with the *tiao–kuai* matrix, these institutions shape governance structures and practices, and their transformations over the course of market reform have resulted in a sea change in the modes of urban governance.

The party and its adaptation

Together with the military and the government, the Chinese Communist Party is one of the three major political hierarchies governing the country. China is a one-party state in spite of the fact that there are eight minority parties in the country. Members of minority parties and non-members can serve in the National People's Congress, but they are in no position to challenge the CCP leadership. Members of minority parties can also join the CCP. Founded in 1921 in Shanghai, the CCP has survived and adapted over nine decades, with 73.36 million members as of the year 2007 (Shambaugh, 2008). Learning from both the failed communist parties in the Soviet bloc and democratic parties in the successful economies of East Asia, the CCP has implemented a number of major reforms since 2004 to improve its governing capacity. Such reform measures include, for example, strengthening party committees at all levels, promoting within-party democracy, combating corruption, and enhancing the career training of party members. During the frequent anti-corruption campaigns, hundreds of thousands of party members have been punished, and some have been stripped of their party membership or even executed. The Chinese term *shuanggui* is probably the most feared word among government officials. It refers to investigations of party officials who break the rules, which often involve torture and sleep-deprived interrogations. Former mayor of Chongqing Bo Xilai and former railway minister Liu Zhijun are recent examples of high-profile party members who have been handed over to party prosecutors.[5] In the mid-2000s, the party began accepting membership applications from private business owners, signaling an attempt to diversify and broaden its support base. The CCP has changed from an institution based on communist ideology and class struggle to a hybrid organization that draws legitimacy mostly from fast-track economic growth.

The position of the Communist Party in the Chinese bureaucracy can be perplexing. On the official Chinese government website, two streams of leadership are listed – *government* leaders and *party* leaders.[6] *Government* executives at all levels – from the Prime Minister, provincial chiefs, and mayors, to township leaders and village heads, are all paired with *party* secretaries, and both posts are equal in rank and decision-making power. Many party secretaries at the city level are actively engaged in promoting economic development. Ultimately, the party hierarchy has authority over its executive counterpart. When party secretaries are caught in corruption cases, only upper-level government units can remove them from their posts. For example, Chen Liangyu, the party secretary of Shanghai (2001–6), oversaw and commissioned numerous mega-projects during his term. He was removed from his party secretary post in 2006 and stripped of party membership by the central government, on charges of corruption and misuse of pension funds. He was sentenced to 18 years in jail.

Danwei *and SOE reform*

Danwei was the major vehicle for the one-party state to govern its urban population during the socialist years. *Danwei* means workplaces, and is often translated in English as "work units." The origins of *danwei* can be traced back to the 1930s, when the Communist Party based its headquarters in Yan'an, in rural Shannxi province, where the communist cadres experimented with new ways of communal living around the idea of "public families" (Bray, 2005). The government reinstated the *danwei* system after the Great Famine (1958–61) in order to effectively control population movement and the allocation of resources. Examples of *danwei* include factories, schools, universities, and enterprises. *Danwei* existed only in urban areas; the equivalent organizational units in rural areas were People's Communes. Unlike in the Soviet Union, which had relatively high occupational mobility, in socialist China it was rare for urban workers to transfer from one *danwei* to another. There was a great deal of variation in size, rank, and wealth among *danwei*, and personal economic well-being largely depended on the power, prestige, and resources of one's *danwei*.

Danwei carried out not only economic but also social functions, acting as key providers and distributors of social welfare goods and services, such as schooling, health care, housing, and food. *Danwei* also served important political and social control functions such as mass mobilization, enforcement of the One-Child policy, and surveillance of everyday life. Most urban residents had a *danwei* affiliation, and the majority lived close to work in *danwei* housing units. Cities in socialist China were spatially organized around *danwei* compounds, many of which had physical walls and fences separating each *danwei* from the others and from the rest of the city.

The *danwei* system has weakened substantially with the reforms of state-owned enterprises (SOEs). SOEs include both state sole-funded corporations and those mixed-ownership enterprises with the state as the biggest shareholder. SOEs were encouraged to shed their social welfare functions and engage in market competition with other enterprises, such as private firms, TVEs, and foreign companies. Many SOEs could not adjust to the reforms and went into bankruptcy, simply abandoning their employees. The remaining SOEs started to lay off their workers, many of whom had worked all their life for their *danwei*. As a result of the SOE reforms, together with other urban reforms in the labor market and housing sector, by the end of the 1990s most *danwei* had stopped allocating free housing to their employees. The once clientelist relationship between *danwei* and lifetime employees has changed into a temporary and contract-based one. Along with welfare provision and job security, the former social control functions of *danwei* over employees and their private lives are gone as well. Most urban residents no longer need to ask permission from their workplace in order to marry, divorce, attend university, and travel, as they did in the socialist years.

SOE reforms were once regarded as an insurmountable task in the overall reform package, but recent studies show that SOE reforms have been largely completed in a quite successful manner (Oi, 2010). Most SOEs were dissolved, downsized, or converted to other ownership forms between 1995 and 2005. In 1998, the SOE sector was still inefficient, employing 122 million workers and running a deep deficit. By 2006, the labor force in the state sector had shrunk to 76 million and the number of SOEs had been reduced massively (Oi, 2010). According to the Second National Economic Census, there were 143,000 SOEs by the end of 2008, down by 20 percent from 2004, while the number of private enterprises had reached 3,596,000, up by 82.4 percent from 2004. Overall, only 3.1 percent of the total number of enterprises were SOEs. The total assets of the corporations engaged in secondary and tertiary industries were 208 trillion RMB, and of this, the share belonging to SOEs was 30 percent.[7] In short, the number of SOEs has decreased sharply over time, but the state sector still controls a significant part – about a third – of the total enterprise assets in China.

The remaining SOEs are a very different group from the socialist *danwei* – they tend to be bigger, more competitive, and more profitable. The SOE reform followed the strategy of "grasping the big, letting go of the small": smaller SOEs were encouraged to file for bankruptcy to reduce the welfare burdens of local governments, while large SOEs were subsidized and super-large SOEs were formed through expansion and mergers. As of 2010, there were only 153 SOEs under the control of the central government (Walder, 2010), but many of them are competitive and some are even listed on international stock exchanges, which was unimaginable in the socialist years. A number of large SOEs have in recent years monopolized key economic sectors such as oil, energy, electricity, transportation, and telecommunications, and some of them have been investing in and merging with companies in other countries. Among the 500 largest Chinese companies in 2011, 316 are SOEs, according to a survey by the China Enterprise Confederation.[8] Table 2.1 shows the 20 largest Chinese companies in 2011, and the list is almost exclusively composed of SOEs. Sinopec (China Petroleum and Chemical Corporation), the largest SOE in the country, is currently listed on the Hong Kong Stock Exchange and trades in New York and Shanghai. Ranking fifth on the Fortune Global 500 list in

Table 2.1: 20 Largest Chinese companies in 2011

2011 RANK	COMPANY NAME	HEAD-QUARTERS	REVENUE (MILLION RMB)	PROFIT (MILLION RMB)	ASSETS (MILLION RMB)	NUMBER OF EMPLOYEES
1	China Petroleum & Chemical Corporation (Sinopec)	Beijing	1,969,042	51,640	1,485,240	640,535
2	China National Petroleum Corporation (CNPC)	Beijing	1,720,885	97,252	2,629,956	1,674,541
3	State Grid Corporation of China	Beijing	1,528,808	32,443	2,077,523	1,564,001
4	Industrial and Commercial Bank of China Limited	Beijing	545,002	166,025	13,458,622	397,339
5	China Mobile Communication Corporation (CMCC)	Beijing	519,016	65,885	1,059,153	207,404
6	China Railway Group Limited	Beijing	473,663	7,488	389,306	285,054

	Company	Location				
7	China Railway Construction Corporation Limited (CRCC)	Beijing	470,159	4,317	350,194	260,268
8	China Construction Bank Corporation (CCB)	Beijing	454,087	134,844	10,810,317	313,867
9	China Life Insurance Company Limited	Beijing	437,523	23,729	1,776,020	118,362
10	Agricultural Bank of China Limited (ABC)	Beijing	407,942	94,873	10,337,406	444,447
11	Bank of China Limited (BOC)	Beijing	400,247	109,691	10,459,865	279,301
12	China State Construction Engineering Corporation	Beijing	370,418	14,715	397,539	123,578
13	Dongfeng Motor Corporation	Hubei	368,834	23,221	217,763	163,990
14	China Southern Power Grid Corporation Limited	Guangdong	368,574	7,719	490,773	323,958

Table 2.1: 20 Largest Chinese companies in 2011 (continued)

2011 RANK	COMPANY NAME	HEAD-QUARTERS	REVENUE (MILLION RMB)	PROFIT (MILLION RMB)	ASSETS (MILLION RMB)	NUMBER OF EMPLOYEES
15	Shanghai Automobile Industry Corporation (SAIC)	Shanghai	367,277	12,956	292,520	109,500
16	China National Offshore Oil Corporation (CNOOC)	Beijing	354,762	74,230	617,200	65,900
17	Sinochem Group	Beijing	335,327	7,344	211,455	50,073
18	FAW Group Corporation	Jilin	294,016	24,859	172,549	84,191
19	China Communications Construction Group	Beijing	273,572	9,437	311,067	103,010
20	Bao Steel Group Corporation	Beijing	272,984	19,877	432,130	104,768

Source: http://www.china.org.cn/business/2011-09/03/content_23344983.htm

2011, Sinopec has set up 12 representative offices in Europe, North America, Southeast Asia, Central Asia, Africa, the Middle East, and the Caribbean, and it has been actively acquiring oil companies in Africa, Canada, and Brazil.[9] Although many SOEs today have transformed themselves into modern corporations, some of the past *danwei* legacies still remain, such as provisions of subsidies for housing and for the education of employees' children.

The hukou *system and recent modifications*

The *hukou* system in China has been extensively studied (see Chan, 1996; Chan and Buckingham, 2008; Chan, 2009). Here it suffices to highlight three of its primary functions in the socialist era: it was a state strategy to restrict population movement between cities and rural areas, to concentrate resources in urban areas in order to promote industrialization, and to exploit the peasantry by unequally distributing welfare resources between the urban and rural sectors. The party and *danwei* would not have been so effective in regulating every aspect of urban life without the *hukou* system. China has had some form of household registration system for more than 1,000 years. In the Song dynasty, the *baojia* system was introduced, which organized households into small groups for social-control purposes. During the Ming period, the *baojia* system was implemented more widely, with 10 households grouped together at the lowest level. Periodic reports of good and bad behavior by families were submitted for social surveillance. Families were required to post a doorplate listing the number and age of their members, along with other information. *Hukou* is the modern reincarnation of the *baojia* system, aimed at social-spatial control of the population.

In the early 1950s, Chinese peasants moved to cities in search of better jobs and opportunities. The limited resources in urban areas for essential welfare provisions such as food, housing, and schools could not meet the demand created by the sharp population increase. In 1958, the central government installed the *hukou* system to prevent population movement between cities and rural areas. The *hukou* system divided the national population into two segments – agricultural and non-agricultural – and residents with agricultural *hukou* were confined to working on the land and denied access to urban social welfare. Peasants could not survive in cities, as jobs, food, education, and health care were provided by the state through *danwei* only to residents with non-agricultural *hukou*.

In spite of the critical role of *hukou* in regulating population movement, surprisingly, the system has rather weak legal foundations. Wang (2004) points out that *hukou* is not backed up by the Constitution, but rather by two fairly obscure administrative regulations passed in 1958 and 1985.[10] The administrator of *hukou* remains the Ministry of Public Security, and its management is decentralized to more than 300,000 police stations across the country. In addition to controlling population movement, *hukou* is also used to manage the "targeted people," also called *zhongdian renkou* (Wang, 2004). The list of "targeted people" has changed over time, but it invariably includes people with criminal records, leaders of religious sects and secret societies, cadres of reactionary parties, and others who are in general believed by the authorities to pose a potential threat to social stability. Wang (2004) argues that although *hukou* has been relaxed to a certain degree, the fundamentals have not changed much since the 1950s. Let us take a look at what has changed and what has not.

In general, the restriction of population movement through *hukou* has been largely relaxed since the 1980s to ensure a ready supply of cheap labor for the manufacturing belt in the south. Migrant workers can acquire a legal residency permit in the cities where they work, which they need to renew periodically to maintain their legal status. Migrants were previously required by law to carry their residency permit, and those without the permit could be detained and sent back to the places of their official registration. This requirement was ended in 2003 by the central government in response to the public outcry after the death of Sun Zhigang. Sun was a student from a Wuhan university who went to Guangzhou to look for work. He was stopped by police for not carrying a temporary residency permit and was beaten to death while in police custody.

There have also been a series of attempts to redirect population movement to smaller cities by offering urban *hukou* status to newcomers. For example, in 1984, the State Council permitted farmers to move to small towns and allowed them to change their *hukou* status from agricultural to non-agricultural; in 2001, the State Council passed a similar policy to allow agricultural *hukou* holders to relocate to small cities and towns with a population of less than 200,000, and to change their *hukou* status accordingly (Ma and Cui, 2002). The State Council also announced that anyone with a stable non-agricultural income and permanent residency in a small city or town for two years could qualify for urban *hukou* (Wang, 2004). But all these reform measures focus on small cities, and it is still beyond the reach of most migrants to get local *hukou* in large cities.

The glass ceiling of *hukou* is, however, lifted for the highly educated, the talented, and the wealthy. For the highly educated and talented – for doctoral degree holders, people who have come back from overseas with foreign university degrees, actors, famed artists, and Olympic medalists – *hukou* is simply not an issue; they can choose to live in any city in the country (Wang, 2004). Some cities offer urban *hukou* to homebuyers and investors who invest a certain amount in real estate and business enterprises. In short, compared to the 1950s, *hukou* has been significantly relaxed to allow population mobility and meet the new demands of market reform, such as attracting investment and talent.

In spite of the various modifications, the core functions of the *hukou* system have not changed much. It is still the single most important institution that divides the country's population into two classes and distributes life opportunities unequally across the rural–urban divide. Chan and Buckingham (2008) argue that *hukou* is not likely to go away in spite of the various signs of reform. They note that the agenda of the *hukou* reforms after 2000 is to devolve the responsibility for *hukou* policies to local governments and let them decide how to incorporate the local agricultural population and migrants from outside into the urban welfare system. As local governments are primarily concerned with economic growth, it is rare to see local initiatives that actively incorporate the rural population and migrants. For example, because migrant children are largely left out of urban public-school systems, in May 2001 the State Council urged local governments to take the responsibility of providing nine years of compulsory education to migrants' children. However, unwilling to bear the additional cost of providing education to these children, few local governments have followed this order from the center. Most urban schools still do not accept migrant children, and the quality of schools for migrant children is much inferior to that of schools for urban children (Kwong, 2004).

There have also been experiments in giving urban *hukou* status to peasants living close to urban areas, but Chan and Buckingham (2008) rightly observe that this is happening in a limited number of places – such as mega-cities and coastal provinces experiencing high-speed development – and most such cases involve land acquisitions. It is a common strategy of city governments to change the *hukou* status of village farmers from rural to urban in order to take their land. In such cases, the farmers automatically lose their collective ownership of the land and, as compensation, they receive urban *hukou* and some welfare benefits. In many cases, farmers are unwilling to let go of their rural *hukou* because land offers a safety net for their livelihood and, in some instances, there is also financial and social gain from holding agricultural *hukou* – such as income from developing and renting out property, dividends from holding shares of village enterprises, and the privilege of having a second child, in some provinces.

CITIES SURROUNDING THE COUNTRYSIDE

Mao's communist revolution succeeded largely because of the land reforms in the countryside and the mobilization of peasants. Large cities were strongholds of Chiang Kai-Shek's Nationalist Party, and only toward the very end of the Nationalist rule, in the late 1940s, did the People's Liberation Army march into large urban centers. Mao Zedong referred to the strategy of rural mass mobilization as *nongcun baowei chengshi*, that is, "surrounding cities with the countryside." The revolutionaries of the 1920s, however, probably did not foresee that after three decades of socialism and another three decades of market reform, China at the beginning of the twenty-first century would embrace an urban revolution, a process in which cities have surrounded the countryside. As power, authority, and resources are devolved from the central to the local level, city governments have become key players in managing local economic affairs. Cities have greatly expanded their physical boundaries by bringing the nearby rural areas under their control.

A number of strategies have been employed by city governments to systematically expand and assert control over rural areas (Ma, 2005; Shen, 2007). The first strategy is to convert entire counties to cities. Between 1983 and 1990, county-level cities more than tripled in number from 133 to 430 – in other words, nearly 300 counties were converted into cities in this period by order of the central government. As county governments climb ranks to become city governments, they gain power and authority to undertake urban construction. Many of the new counties-turned-cities are still dominated by a large rural sector, and their landscape exhibits a mixture of both urban and rural features. Second, some cities have received consent from the central government to bring the surrounding counties under their control, an arrangement referred to as "cities administering counties." In the process, the power of the counties is substantially reduced, and this has created conflicts between city and county authorities. City officials tend to adopt policies that favor the development of central city areas at the expense of counties, such as acquiring land and food supply from counties, retaining funds allocated from the central government, and competing with counties over raw materials, investment, and development projects. Third, cities have also been aggressively annexing counties. In this case, the counties are turned into urban districts. Many large cities such as Guangzhou, Wuhan, Shenzhen, Shanghai, and Beijing have used this strategy to expand outward physically, acquiring more land in order to relocate heavy industries from inner cities, to relieve population pressure, and to engage in new rounds of property development. In Shanghai, foreign-themed residential new towns have quickly replaced former agricultural fields in the newly annexed urban districts (see chapter 3).

The vast hinterland of counties thus offers more space for cities to sprawl outwards, both physically and administratively. The above strategies clearly put rural counties in a disadvantaged position and further enhance the power of city governments.

LAND GOVERNANCE

In the early 1990s, the Pudong area of Shanghai was still dominated by rice fields, and the East Third Ring Road area in Beijing was occupied by large manufacturing facilities and dilapidated *danwei* housing. A decade later, farmers, workers, and manufacturing facilities had all gone, and both places have now become the major Central Business

Districts in the country, with massive construction of office skyscrapers, luxury high-rises, and state-of-the-art infrastructure. The transformation of the built environment would not have been possible without the reforms in the land governance system in the 1980s, which separated public land ownership from private land-use rights. Since then the regulation of the land sector has gone through further modifications, reflecting the intensifying inter-scalar conflicts among different levels of government and central ministries.

Public land ownership vs private land-use rights

Land was not a commodity in the socialist period. It was allocated by the state to *danwei* and for specific industrial projects. Article 10 of the 1982 Constitution specifies that no organization or individual may seize and sell land or make any other unlawful transfer of land (Yeh and Wu, 1996). In the early days of market reform, governments were short of capital to build infrastructure and attract foreign investors, and some coastal cities such as Shenzhen began to experiment with privatization of land-use rights. In the early phase of the land reform, before the mid-1980s, the main agenda was to provide cheap land to foreign investors to induce them to help build infrastructure. The experiment in the south went well, and investors from Hong Kong and Taiwan flocked to the Special Economic Zones to set up factories and take advantage of the cheap land.

To expand the land reform to other cities, in 1998 the Constitution was amended with the clause, "the right to use land may be transferred in accordance with the provisions of law." Thus, the Constitution recognized market transactions of land-use rights for the first time. Land-use rights are separated from land ownership, the former being privatized and the latter remaining public. Individual and institutional investors can obtain land-use rights for up to 70 years for residential use, and 50 years for commercial use. The agenda for privatizing land-use rights has changed since the late 1990s, from giving incentives to investors to provide infrastructure to generating local government revenues. According to the current fiscal policies, revenues from leasing land are counted as "extra-budgetary" and do not have to be shared with the central government. As land is leased by local governments to private parties, and transacted among investors, land-leasing and transaction fees have become a major source of municipal government revenue. Part of the revenue obtained from land leasing is used by governments to improve infrastructure, which can in turn enhance accessibility and open up more land on the urban fringes for development.

Land-leasing

The hybrid land market in China, with public ownership and private use rights, has been operating with a multi-track system in which land is transacted both through under-the-table negotiations between the government and private investors and through public auctions. It has been common practice for local governments to transfer land-use rights through negotiations. To improve market transparency, the central government has urged that all commercial land be transferred publicly through auctions to the highest bidder but, in practice, due to the intertwined interests of local governments and investors, under-the-table negotiations remain the dominant method of land leasing. Many officials and their relatives are shareholders in real-estate companies and construction projects, and local governments commonly lease out land at prices far below market value to these enterprises with strong government ties. Local governments prefer negotiations to auctions because this method allows them to attract investors by lowering land prices (Xu, Yeh, and Wu, 2009). Good connections with local governments are crucial for individuals and companies trying to obtain prime land at a fraction of its market price.

Land seizures

Urban land is owned by the state and rural land by village collectives. The state has the right, according to the current Constitution, to acquire rural land from farmers and urban land from its current users in the name of the public interest. In most cases, farmers and urban residents are compensated by local governments at rates far below the market prices that investors would pay to those governments to acquire the same land, and the local governments can easily pocket huge profits through land transactions – by acquiring land cheaply and then leasing it to investors. State expropriation of land takes many forms, from violent means such as mobilization of armed forces and forced demolitions to administrative means such as manipulation of the *hukou* system.

Land grabs by city governments are widespread and have generated serious conflict. In 2005, in the small village of Dongzhou in Guangdong province, the local government decided to expropriate land from farmers and build a power plant. Unsatisfied with the insufficient compensation and worried about environmental damage to crops, angry farmers took their grievance to the streets. Armed police, mobilized by the local government, opened fire on the protestors, killing a dozen villagers and wounding many more. This was the first time that armed forces had opened fire on civilians since the 1989 Tian'anmen student movement.[11] In 2011, in Wukan, another village in Guangdong, villagers stormed into government offices, chased away local officials, and blocked the roads after they learned that the village government had leased out about a third of the village land to an outside investor. One of the representatives chosen by the villagers to negotiate with the village government had died in police custody. The stand-off between the villagers and security forces sent by local authorities continued for months. Finally, in 2012, the Guangdong provincial government intervened. The formal village officials were dismissed, the land deal was put on hold, and the villagers were allowed to hold elections to choose new leaders. The Wukan protest marked a turning point in Chinese peasants' resistance against land grabs.[12]

Land expropriation can also be accomplished by changing the *hukou* status of farmers. In 2004, Shenzhen converted 235 square kilometers of rural land to urban land in Bao'an and Longgang districts by reclassifying the *hukou* status of villagers from "agricultural" to "non-agricultural." After becoming "non-agricultural" *hukou* holders, villagers are no longer entitled to rural land, and village collectives are abolished. Farmers are often compensated at rates far below market prices, and governments apply the majority of the compensation to buying pensions and medical insurance for the farmers, and the rest to building community facilities (Xu, Yeh, and Wu, 2009). In the Chongqing case, discussed earlier in this chapter, farmers received only 250 RMB in cash to cover transition expenses. The strategy of acquiring farmers' land by offering them urban *hukou* is widely pursued by many large cities. In 2005, there were 70,000 such proposals by local governments (Xu, Yeh, and Wu, 2009).

In general, villagers have little power and resources to resist land grabs by the state but, occasionally, powerful villages are able to reject offers by local governments and villagers can refuse to change their rural *hukou* status to urban, as happened in the early phase of the Villages-in-Cities (ViCs) developments in Shenzhen. Farmers in Shenzhen are reluctant to let go of their rural *hukou*; some have become powerful landlords by building housing on the collectively owned village land and renting rooms to migrants (see chapter 4).

The reign of ministries

Due to concerns over the rapid conversion of arable land, food security, and protests by landless farmers, the central government has begun to tighten its regulation of the land market. This move indicates a new phase of land governance, characterized by the central government's effort to restrain the power and authority previously granted to city governments. Scholars point out that this is evidence of the recentralization of power in the central government (Xu and Yeh, 2009).

In 1998, the central government established the Ministry of Land and Resources by merging a number of bureaus; the new ministry oversees the planning, management, and conservation of land nationwide. In the same year, the Land Administration Law was modified to reduce the power of municipal governments in land acquisitions. For example, any acquisition of agricultural land has to be approved by the State Council; cities can only grant land-use rights to private parties from a quota of land that has been designated for construction; and urban districts no longer have any legal power in land administration (Xu and Yeh, 2009). This reconsolidation of authority in the hands of the Ministry of Land and Resources has helped to prevent the rapid conversion of arable land for rural housing construction, but has not been effective in preventing the conversion of agricultural land for industrial and urban development (Lin and Ho, 2005). Lin (2009) notes that local government officials routinely underreport the amount of available land under their jurisdiction and often classify fertile farmland in good locations as wasteland so they can later lease it out to investors. To get accurate statistics, the central government has begun conducting land surveys across the country with the help of state-of-the-art satellite remote-sensing technologies.

In spite of its various attempts to cool land-development fever, the regulatory power of the Ministry of Land and Resources is still largely uncertain, and the incidence of illegal use of land continues to increase. In the first three months of 2011, the ministry found close to 10,000 cases of illegal use of land – most of which were acknowledged, supported, or even initiated by local governments.[13] In June 2011, the central government released the names of 73 officials in local governments and ministries of land under whose jurisdiction illegal use of land was discovered. In some cases, the listed officials were demoted to lower-rank positions.[14] Efforts to regulate land development are often resisted by local governments since land-leasing fees are a major source of government revenues.

The last resort for the central government to reassert its power over land governance seems to be the targeted appointment of local officials. Since 2003, the key officials in local land departments have been appointed by land departments at the next higher level rather than by local governments themselves (Xu and Yeh, 2009). For example, instead of the Mayor and Party Secretary of Shanghai appointing the officials in charge of land development in the city, the Ministry of Land and Resources does so directly. But the appointed land officials often find themselves constrained by other local departments, and have to modify the orders from above. Therefore, even with its intervention through personnel appointments, the center still has limited power to control land administration at the local level.

Enterprising local governments

Local governments, from the province level to the village level, have become increasingly innovative in finding ways to make land available for development in spite of the tight regulation by the central government. Yang and Wang (2008) examined how local governments had used land to attract investment in Suzhou and the two nearby cities of Kunshan and Wujiang. Suzhou has established several industrial parks to attract foreign capital, such as Suzhou-Singapore Industrial Park, Suzhou New District, and Kunshan-Wujiang Economic Development Area. These various industrial parks and special zones have attracted a large amount of capital investment from the Taiwanese electronics industry. Yang and Wang (2008) reported that most local officials in Suzhou region considered land quota allocations from upper-level governments – intended to restrict the amount of arable land that can be converted to non-agricultural use every year – as nuisances to avoid. Local officials always approved development projects and assured investors that land was available. In another study, Wang et al. (2010) reported that local governments in Zhejiang province were experimenting with the transfer of land development rights between rich and poor counties to avoid the quotas imposed by the central government. Rich counties bought land-use quotas from poor counties and, with financial compensation, poor counties cultivated new farmland through consolidation or reclamation of waste and construction land. Jinyun county, a poor area in Zhejiang, gained 281 million RMB from trading land quotas in 2006; its total revenue for the year was 285 million (Wang et al., 2010).

The privatization of land-use rights has facilitated the devolution of state power from the center to the local level, as most land transactions take place locally and deals are made among private investors, city governments, and the former socialist "land masters" such as SOEs, the military, and party units (Hsing, 2006). But alongside the decentralization, there has been renewed intervention by the central government in land administration, by means of setting up new ministries in charge of land, taking back certain authorities from city governments, and directly appointing local land officials (Xu and Yeh, 2009; Xu, Yeh, and Wu, 2009). Both the decentralization and recentralization arguments are supported by empirical evidence. Land governance practices reflect the strengthened capacity of both the central and local governments in using land – a state asset in China by definition – to facilitate capital accumulation. Power lies everywhere you look in the state hierarchy, from the central government at the top, down to city and district governments. The inter-scalar conflicts reflect the different interests of central and local authorities. For the central government, the main concerns are food security, peasant unrest, and social stability, while for local governments, the main concern is GDP growth, the basis on which local officials get promoted. Outside the state power apparatus are a large number of dispossessed citizens, who have lost land and homes in the spiral of capital accumulation that benefits only a few.

HOUSING GOVERNANCE

Housing reform in China began in the early 1980s. The initial goal was to privatize housing in order to rescue SOEs from their heavy financial burden of providing housing to employees and to make them more competitive (Wang and Murie, 1996, 2000). Under socialism, investment in housing construction was highly centralized and *danwei* played a key role in housing provision. *Danwei* allocated housing free of charge to employees and their families, based on administrative rank, job performance, loyalty, party membership, and connections with officials. The first phase of the reform, in the 1980s and 1990s, was characterized by the selling of *danwei* housing to sitting tenants at substantially subsidized prices. The privatization of public housing in this period was slow, as urban workers either lacked the capital to buy or were reluctant to pay money for the apartments that they had occupied for years at no charge. The allocation of public housing through *danwei* ended in 1998, at least in theory, when the central government issued a special document to forbid provision of free housing and to encourage the development of a private housing market (State Council, 1998). The second phase of the reform, from 1998 to 2005, was characterized by the commoditization of housing, with both *danwei* and private developers making housing stock available to be purchased at market prices. The costs of housing provision were shared by three parties – local governments, *danwei*, and individual homebuyers – with individuals bearing an increasing share. The 1998 policy also introduced a housing finance system to help developers and households access bank loans and mortgages. The development of mortgages was vital to the reform, since it expanded the purchasing power of homebuyers but, at the same time, it also inflated housing prices.

The impact of housing reform on Chinese society cannot be over-stated. It has completely changed how urban Chinese live and their relationship with the most intimate space – the home. Every urban family has a story to tell. A personal story below will illustrate the transition of Chinese citizens from public-housing tenants to private homeowners.

(More than) a place of one's own

My family lived in Harbin in the northeast region of the country, an area that received massive state investment in the socialist years and was hit the hardest during the reform of SOEs in the 1990s. My father worked for a large SOE, which, during its peak years in the 1960s, had hired tens of thousands of workers and provided a wide range of welfare services to employees and their families, such as kindergartens, elementary schools, community colleges, hospitals, cinemas, and, most importantly, free housing. Due to a shortage of housing, there was a long queue of people waiting to be allocated a flat. When my father began working for the company in the mid-1970s, housing was not immediately available and the wait seemed eternal. So my family joined 10 other families and, with a green light from the *danwei* authority, they built a row of one-story houses by themselves on a piece of land owned by the work unit. Compared to the crowded apartment build-ings built by *danwei*, where families often had to share kitchens and bathrooms, the homes in our neighborhood of a dozen families had more space – a front yard for vegetables and flowers, a backyard for kids to play in, and three to four rooms of decent size.

In the late 1980s, the work unit allocated my family a one-bedroom apartment in a modern apartment building. The apartment was small for a family of four, but at least we had a private kitchen and bathroom. Another 10 years passed and, by the late 1990s, the work unit was in bad financial shape. It began to lay off workers and stopped providing any housing for employees. In the meantime, housing reform had begun in the city, and public-housing tenants were encouraged to purchase their apartments. My family bought the one-bedroom apartment from the work unit at a heavily subsidized price. Soon my father left the state company and joined a private firm, and we purchased a two-bedroom apartment in another neighborhood. We had more space this time but did not know our neighbors any more.

In the early 2000s, our first home (the self-constructed one-story house) and second home (the allocated one-bedroom *danwei* apartment) were both demolished because the company sold the land to developers. Also gone was the entire neighborhood of my childhood, with kindergartens, schools, playgrounds, public bathhouses, cultural centers, and cinemas. My family did not receive any compensation for the first home because of its gray legal status, but received some compensation for the second one, because we had bought the place before the demolition. By this time, the privatization of housing in the city was almost complete and, like other families, my parents began to think of retiring to the warmer south and buying more properties as investments. During my annual visits back to China from the States, buying properties has become a main topic for dinner-table discussions. In 2009, my parents bought two flats in Haikou, the capital of Hainan province – 5,000 kilometers away from where they live. And in 2010, after a trip to coastal Shandong province, which has a mild climate, my parents bought another two flats in a new housing development there that targets "snow birds" from the north.

From a self-constructed house in a work-unit compound, to five apartments in three cities in north, central, and south China, the story of my family tells the story of the country's housing-market boom. According to the Ministry of Housing, by 2010, 72.8 percent of urban Chinese families owned residential properties, and the average living area per capita increased from 6.7 square meters in 1978 to 30 square meters in 2008.[15] Because of rising incomes, a lack of investment outlets, and an inadequate social safety net, urban Chinese families not only have bought private homes to live in, but also have come to see real estate as an investment.

Roaring housing prices and central policies

With the privatization of housing and more money pouring into the property sector, inflation in housing prices has quickly gotten out of control. Especially in first-tier cities such as Beijing, Shanghai, Shenzhen, and Suzhou, housing prices doubled or even tripled in the 2000s. According to the National Bureau of Statistics, in April 2010, housing prices in 70 large and medium-sized cities were on average 12.8 percent higher than in April 2009. The sharpest jumps were observed in Haikou and Sanya in the special economic zone of Hainan province, which recorded increases of 64.3 percent and 58.2 percent. Even in Beijing and Shenzhen, where housing had already become unaffordable for many, the prices had still jumped by 21.5 percent and 21.3 percent during the previous year.[16] Between 2001 and 2010, average residential property prices in Beijing increased by more than 300 percent (figure 2.2).

The overheating of the housing market in China is in sharp contrast with the market in the United States, where property prices hit a historic low after the mortgage default crisis in 2008. Policymakers in China are pressed to find solutions to cool down the housing market and curb the roaring housing prices. In 2005, the State Council issued an urgent notice calling for the stabilization of housing prices and asking local governments to take actions to make housing more affordable.

The central government has experimented with a vast number of ad hoc policies, such as tightening bank credit, increasing the housing supply, and introducing a property-tax system, which China still did not have in 2012. The Bank of China raised interest rates three times

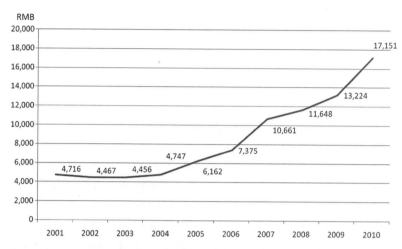

Figure 2.2 Housing prices in Beijing, 2001–2010
Source: China Statistical Yearbooks, 2002–2011.
Note: The numbers are average selling prices of residential properties, including both luxury and low-income housing (i.e., Economic and Comfortable Housing, or *jingji shiyong fang*) and excluding offices and commercial properties.

in 2011, to a high of 3.5 percent, in order to fight inflation and make loans more expensive for homebuyers and developers. The government also raised down payments from 20 percent to 30 percent for first-time homebuyers, and to 50 percent for second-home buyers. To increase the housing supply, the central government ordered local governments to provide 3 million units of affordable housing for lower-income families in 2010 and another 10 million units in 2011. Large-scale demolitions and evictions have been halted because they were the main source of demand for new housing, for those who are relocated. SOEs with real-estate operations have been ordered to step back from property development. In terms of taxation, there has been an experiment in collecting property tax in selected cities, such as Shanghai and

Chongqing, to discourage investment in property. Lastly, similar to the central government's approach to land governance, there has been an attempt to control housing prices through personnel appointments – the promotion of local officials can be affected if housing prices in their cities rise too fast and too high. It is unclear how effective this last measure is.

Local non-cooperation

The central policies for cooling down the housing market have met heavy resistance from local governments, as local revenues largely depend on a strong and speculative housing market. Local governments have announced their own policies to demonstrate that they are committed to controlling housing prices as well, but many of these local policies either are ineffective or have led to unanticipated results. For example, Shanghai announced in 2010 that each individual family could buy only one apartment. Following the announcement, there was an immediate drop in the number of marriage registrations, as young couples wanted to delay their marriage so they could buy two flats instead of one. In Beijing, the government announced that only those who had been living and paying taxes in the city for five consecutive years could buy property, to prevent binge-buying by speculators, but the policy also excludes migrant professional workers and has no effect on speculative capital poured directly into housing construction. The initiative of collecting property tax has met resistance from all fronts – from middle-class homeowners to local governments. As two of the cities chosen as experimental sites, Shanghai and Chongqing decided on a tax rate lower than 1 percent of a home's value, and it only applies to luxury homes, which make up a small percentage of the housing market. The central government's affordable-housing program, if realized, would significantly reduce the demand for housing in the private sector. But the plan will not be realized without cooperation from city governments. Most city governments have overspent on infrastructure and lack incentives to build housing for the poor.

Overall, the governance of housing has gone through three major phases in the market-reform period. The first phase (1980–97) was marked by the selling of public-housing stock to current tenants; the second phase (1998–2005) saw the formation of a private-housing market and the abolition of the free allocation of housing by work units; and the current phase (2005–present) is characterized by efforts by the central government to rein in inflation in housing prices and to make housing more affordable. These efforts have been largely unsuccessful for a variety of reasons. Central regulations have met strong resistance from local governments and have had no substantial effects. Local governments, as long as their revenue is tied to the real-estate sector, lack incentives to pass policies that will cool down the housing sector. For the central government, the dilemma lies in how to balance promoting economic growth with addressing social inequality, and, when economic growth is threatened, the central government has always chosen to make policies that stimulate the economy. In 2003, right after the SARS crisis, the central government announced that the real-estate sector was one of the "pillar industries" of the economy, and revised its previous promise to "provide affordable housing for 70 to 80 percent of families" to a statement that "the majority of families should purchase or rent housing on the market" (State Council, 2003). After the global financial crisis in 2008, the real-estate market in China cooled down significantly, and the central government loosened regulations and issued new policies to encourage more investment in the real-estate and housing sector. Additionally, middle-class homeowners form a strong interest group that does not want to see housing prices go down. There are frequent newspaper stories about angry homeowners storming into sales offices protesting against developers slashing prices.[17]

The transformation of the land and housing sectors reveals the changing regime of urban governance in contemporary China, from a highly centralized system prioritizing national economic development to a decentralized system in which the interests of empowered and pro-growth local governments often clash with those of the central government and ministries.

INFRASTRUCTURE AND PUBLIC–PRIVATE PARTNERSHIP

China has been exceptional among developing countries in its investments in urban infrastructure. Cities have invested massive amounts to build public utilities, roads, bridges, tunnels, parks, sanitation services, ports, airports, and subways. To minimize the negative effects of the 2008 world financial crisis, the central government announced a large stimulus package to encourage investment in the infrastructure sector, and local governments eagerly responded with ambitious investment plans. The spending on fixed-asset investment – a measure that captures building activities such as real-estate and infrastructure construction, among other things – has reached an alarming 70 percent of the national GDP, and infrastructure spending has passed foreign trade as the biggest contributor to national economic growth.[18] Across the country, local governments have been on a building binge because the promotion of local officials is still tied to short-term economic growth that is heavily dependent on infrastructure and real-estate activities. Many municipal governments have incurred huge debts in order to finance their ambitious infrastructure projects, but the debts often do not show up in the official balance sheet, as local governments set up investment companies through which to raise capital.

The regional pattern of infrastructure development is largely uneven, corresponding to the development gaps between the eastern, central, and western regions. Cities in the eastern region have the most developed urban infrastructure and more resources to finance their infrastructure projects, while cities in the western interior have fewer resources and find themselves in deeper debt as they emulate Beijing and Shanghai by building state-of-the-art subways, expressways, and extravagant government buildings.

Financing infrastructure

How some local governments in China can invest so much in building infrastructure is often a puzzle for both specialists and casual observers of Chinese cities. The mechanisms of financing urban infrastructure in China have changed over time. The role of work units in providing infrastructure has diminished and, in their place, municipal governments have taken on a key position. Most municipalities do not have sufficient tax revenue – for example, they do not collect property taxes – to finance their ambitious infrastructure projects. Most properties are still owned by the public sector, and local governments are reluctant to tax their own assets and share the tax revenue with the central government. Moreover, the propertied middle class resists any policy experiments to impose property taxes. Given the limited local tax revenues and diminishing subsidies from the central government, extra-budgetary revenues and borrowing from the capital market have become major sources of infrastructure financing (Wu, 2010a).

Extra-budgetary revenues refer to those municipal incomes that do not come directly from taxes, but are derived from various fees charged to enterprises. Wu (2010a) finds that the Shanghai city government charges more than 28 kinds of fees to real-estate investors and that this extra-budgetary income accounts for up to 25 percent of infrastructure investment funds. Income from land leasing also counts as extra-budgetary revenue and has become the most significant source of revenue for local governments. In 2010, the city governments of Shanghai and

Beijing pocketed more than 100 billion RMB from the leasing of land to developers – income that did not have to be shared with the central government.[19]

Moreover, borrowing from domestic and foreign capital markets through bonds, equities, loans from state-run banks, stock-market listings, and joint ventures has become a new way to raise funds, accounting for more than 30 percent of infrastructure investment capital (Wu, 2010a). Among these types of borrowing, loans from state-run banks have become the main method for municipal governments to finance their ambitious infrastructure projects. As the central government has tightened requirements for state-run banks' lending to municipal governments, special-purpose investment platforms have been set up to evade these regulations. According to some estimates, by 2011, more than 10,000 platforms in capital markets had been set up by local governments to raise funds for investing in infrastructure.[20] Bank loans do not go directly to municipalities, but go instead to the accounts of these investment companies that finance the construction of roads, bridges, subways, and government offices. City-owned land valued at high prices is used as collateral for these loan deals. In this way, the debt incurred does not show up on the municipalities' balance sheets. Most of the investment platforms set up by local governments are deeply in debt. For example, the Urban Construction Investment and Development Corporation of Wuhan – the capital city of Hubei province – has 15 billion USD in registered assets but 14 billion USD in debt. The total local-government debt in the country was estimated to range between 2 and 3 trillion USD in 2011, which was about a third of China's GDP that year.[21] State-run banks are eager to lend to investment platforms set up by local governments because of high potential returns, in spite of warnings from financial regulators in Beijing about the increasing risks from these hefty infrastructure loans.

For-profit infrastructure

Build-Operate-Transfer (BOT) is a widely adopted model for building roads and bridges. The costs are shared between private investors and local governments, and, after the initial investments are recovered through toll charges, the ownership rights are transferred to local governments. Although BOT has proved to be effective at tapping into the private market to finance infrastructure, by charging exorbitant fees to users, it has turned various infrastructure projects into profit-making machines for local governments and their private partners. For instance, out of a world total of 140,000 toll roads, 100,000 are found in China.[22] Owning and driving a car is a symbol of middle-class living in China, but it has also become costly with the endless toll road charges. The roaring increase in toll charges for roads and bridges has also contributed to the inflation of food prices, as meat and vegetables have to be trucked into cities on a daily basis via toll roads. In June 2011, responding to public outcry over the country's toll system, the central government mobilized five ministries to launch a year-long campaign attempting to eliminate unauthorized toll booths and legal booths that are continuing to operate beyond their authorization period. The campaign has met strong resistance from local authorities.[23]

The Guangdong–Shenzhen Expressway is a prime example of for-profit infrastructure. The expressway is often referred to as the "highest-profit road in China." It is a joint venture of the Guangdong provincial government and Gordon Wu of Hopewell Ltd from Hong Kong. The initial investment, shared by the two parties, was 12.2 billion RMB. The highway connects Guangzhou and Shenzhen, two urban areas with over 20 million people, and it also passes by the city of Dongguan – a manufacturing hub at the heart of the Pearl River Delta with over 8 million people. Because of its route, the highway is always in great demand, and the toll-charge income since its opening in 1997 had exceeded 35 billion RMB by 2011. The owners of the highway – the Guangdong provincial government and Hopewell – are still charging users and have been increasing the toll year after year. The Guangdong provincial government takes in 52.5 percent of the toll income, and Hopewell takes in the remaining 47.5 percent. In spite of the fact that it is a toll road, the services along it are bad – for a period right after it was opened, there were no gas stations for its entire length of 75 miles, and the owners were taken to court for the lack of service provision. The initial planned capacity of the expressway was 80,000 cars per day, but by 2009 the actual traffic had increased to 389,000 cars per day.[24] In spite of public complaints about the toll charges and congestion, the Guangdong provincial government is unwilling to stop charging users or to lower the toll because it is the main beneficiary of the toll collection.

In booming economic regions such as the Pearl River Delta, large infrastructure projects are in high demand, and they often become extremely profitable for investors, but in the less-developed regions in the west, local governments often find themselves unable to repay their huge infrastructure loans. Yunnan province in the southwest embarked on a massive highway construction project during the eleventh Five-Year Plan period. From 2006 to 2010, the province doubled the length of its road network to 206,700 kilometers, making it currently the third longest stretch of highway in the country. Yunnan is among the poorest provinces in China, with a per capita GDP of 2,320 USD in 2010, ranking twenty-fourth nationwide. The vast expressway network remained mostly empty after completion, due to the province's lagging economic development and low population density. Unlike the Guangzhou–Shenzhen Expressway, highways in Yunnan are unable to generate enough profits with toll charges to pay back the loans used to build them. Yunnan Highway Development Investment Limited, an investment platform set up by the provincial government, has a standing loan of more than 100 billion RMB from a dozen state banks, including China Construction Bank, China Development Bank, and the Industrial and Commercial Bank of China. In April 2011, Yunnan Highway informed the banks that it would repay interest but not principal. The banks sent a team of negotiators overnight to the capital city of Kunming to try to restructure the debt. The provincial government is eager to back Yunnan Highway, but finds itself increasingly unable to do so.[25]

Chinese cities have made remarkable progress in building urban infrastructure by tapping into private capital from both domestic and foreign sources. The massive investment in infrastructure has been made possible through public–private partnership and non-transparent platforms for fund-raising. Many infrastructure projects are profit-making machines for both local governments and private investors. But, as local governments prove unable to repay their infrastructure loans, the growth model based on infrastructure investment poses a major threat to China's long-term economic health.

GOVERNING MEGA-CITY REGIONS: THE PEARL RIVER DELTA

Mega-city regions are clusters of continuous metropolitan areas. The major mega-city regions in China are found in the Pearl River Delta and the Yangtze River Delta, each with a population of more than 50 million. Currently, there are no formal institutional structures guiding region-wide planning in mega-city regions, and the horizontal networks among cities have always been weak. Due to the fragmented governance structure in mega-city regions, inter-city competition has intensified and led to the duplication of infrastructure projects, land encroachments, and environmental degradation (Xu and Yeh, 2010). The cut-throat competition for capital investment has had a devastating impact on localities, and a new institutional architecture for inter-city cooperation is urgently needed to coordinate land use, reduce social inequality, and provide environmental protection. Recently, there has been increasing policy attention to developing mega-city region governance structures, such as the 2008 Urban and Rural Planning Law that subjects mega-city regions to formal master planning. Geographers Jiang Xu and Anthony Yeh interpret this renewed interest as an attempt on the part of the central government to regain the authority it lost in the process of decentralization and to help strategically position mega-city regions in the national and international marketplaces. Provincial governments are in favor of the new effort to coordinate regional urban governance, since they can control funding allocated by the central government for key industrial projects in mega-city regions (Xu and Yeh, 2010).

The Pearl River Delta is the most studied mega-city region in China. It covers an area of 54,744 square kilometers in Guangdong province, Hong Kong, and Macau, and has a resident population of over 60 million (Xu and Yeh, 2010). There are nine municipalities of different rank, including Guangzhou – the capital city of Guangdong province, Shenzhen and Zhuhai Special Economic Zones (SEZs), Macau and Hong Kong Special Administrative Regions, and a number of other cities of lower rank such as Zhongshan and Dongguan (figure 2.3). The Pearl River Delta region has the most fragmented governance structure and the fiercest inter-city competition in China, as evidenced by the duplication in airport construction. There are five major airports in the Pearl River Delta, in Hong Kong, Shenzhen, Guangzhou, Macau and Zhuhai, which compete with one another for cargo and passenger traffic. Zhuhai Airport is notorious for its low volume of air traffic. For a period the airport handled no more than a dozen flights per day. Hong Kong is the dominant regional hub, but other cities in the region are reluctant to recognize it and have never incorporated Hong Kong into the regional planning for the Greater Pearl River Delta (Yang, 2006). Guangzhou was historically the leading city in Guangdong province, but, after Shenzhen's spectacular rise in the 1980s, Guangzhou

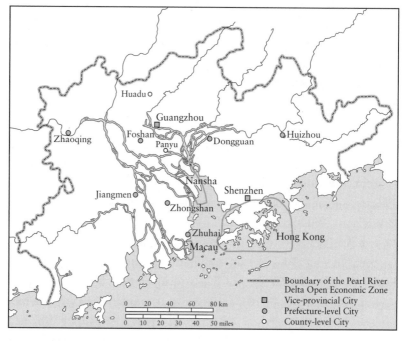

Figure 2.3 Map of the Pearl River Delta

has lagged behind somewhat. Nevertheless, the city is eager to catch up, with ambitious plans to build a Central Business District, expand Baiyun International Airport, annex the neighboring cities of Panyu and Huadu, and build a heavy industrial base and deep-water port in Nansha on the northeast shoreline – though this is an ecologically fragile area.

The fragmentation of region-wide governance and the inter-urban competition in the Pearl River Delta are best illustrated in a case study by geographer Chun Yang on the Hong Kong–Zhuhai–Macau Bridge project connecting Hong Kong to the western Pearl River Delta (Yang, 2006). The western part of the Pearl River Delta has always lagged behind the eastern part, and it is increasingly recognized by Hong Kong investors as the new frontier for investment. But there are no transportation links connecting Hong Kong and the western Pearl River Delta except for ferries or a land detour through the eastern Pearl River Delta. In 1983, Gordon Wu of Hopewell Ltd – the same company that built the Guangzhou–Shenzhen Expressway – proposed to build a bridge connecting Hong Kong and Zhuhai. The proposal was shelved by the central government because of the strained relationship between the local leader of Zhuhai and the central government. Since then multiple proposals have been presented by different city governments, consultants, and private investors. For instance, in 2002, the Guangdong provincial government proposed to build a tunnel connecting Zhuhai and Zhongshan, thus bypassing Hong Kong; in the same year, there was a second, joint proposal between Hopewell and the Guangdong government to build a bridge connecting Hong Kong, Zhuhai, Macau, and Shenzhen; and, in 2006, the Shenzhen government proposed yet another plan, to build a bridge between Shenzhen and Zhongshan. Each of the six parties – the Guangdong provincial government, and the Guangzhou, Zhuhai, Shenzhen, Macau, and Hong Kong governments – hope to make the bridge work for its own interests, and each of the five municipalities want the bridge to help them better compete with others in the region.

The history of the proposals to build a Hong Kong–Zhuhai–Macau Bridge illustrates the persistent inter-city competition within megacity regions and the difficulty of building a region-wide governance structure. There have been a number of strategic plans for promoting horizontal urban networks and inter-city cooperation, but implementation of these plans is often difficult, if not impossible. As Xu and Yeh (2010) point out, the central and provincial governments make strategic plans for the purpose of reasserting their authority in regional governance, rather than to coordinate different interest groups within regions. In addition to strategic plans, some informal platforms have been developed, such as mayors' forums, but the effects of these soft regional alliances are still largely unknown (Wu and Zhang 2010).

COMMUNITY GOVERNANCE

Community (*shequ*) is a new institution of urban governance introduced in the mid-1990s in the course of SOE reforms. According to the Ministry of Civil Affairs, the community was introduced to replace the two lowest levels in the system of urban governance – Street Offices and Resident Committees. Both were established in the socialist period to deliver welfare services to marginalized urban populations, such as the elderly, the disabled, and the unemployed. The majority of the urban population was affiliated with work units, and their social welfare needs were primarily taken care of by their *danwei*. Compared to *danwei*, Street Offices and Resident Committees had fewer resources and more limited power. The situation changed in the mid-1990s as *danwei* began to dissolve and ceased to be providers of social welfare goods and services. At the same time, urban family structures began to change, bringing a rise in the number of divorced couples, single-parent families, elderly people living alone, and working couples, who would need a range of social services that were once provided by work units. The new institution of the community was created to fill the void left by work units and meet the urgent demand for social services.

Community as a socio-spatial institution

Bray (2006) notes that, unlike the western notion of community, the Chinese community has a very specific meaning and clear functions defined by the government. It is designated by the state as the basic unit of urban social, political, and administrative organization. The community is designed to be a partner of the state in implementing policy programs and helping to provide services through market channels. In the first phase of its institutionalization, from the mid-1980s to the mid-1990s, the community was seen as a replacement for the former Resident Committees, delivering social welfare services to residents. With funding from urban district governments, many neighborhoods built new community centers to provide space for services, many of which were outsourced to private providers. In some of the well-financed urban districts, one can find gigantic multi-story community centers, located right in the middle of a neighborhood, offering space for a variety of services and cultural and entertainment activities, such as childcare, post offices, banks, libraries, Ping-Pong rooms, calligraphy rooms, recording studios, computer labs, and dance halls. Since the late 1990s, the community is no longer confined to being a service provider; its functions have been broadened to also include moral education, government propaganda, policing and security, and Party-building. Unlike the former Resident Committees, staffed by retirees and elderly female volunteers, the new community administration is managed by younger and better-educated personnel (Bray, 2006). The community has different penetrative power across neighborhoods. In general, community organizations are weaker in wealthy neighborhoods than in middle- and lower-income neighborhoods, because wealthy residents have more resources at their disposal and less need to rely upon services provided through community associations.

The new community is not only an administrative unit, but also a spatial unit with clearly defined boundaries corresponding to *xiaoqu* – residential compounds (Tomba, 2005; Bray, 2008). Most residents of Chinese cities, regardless of their socio-economic status, live in some type of *xiaoqu*. *Xiaoqu* are typically designed to be closed spatial units, with fences, walls, and security guards, and, in the more upscale *xiaoqu*, surveillance technologies such as swipe cards, CCTV cameras, and monitor rooms are ubiquitous. The entrances of these *xiaoqu* are guarded; most of the time the security guards do not stop visitors to ask for ID, but they do recognize most peddlers, vendors, and rural migrant workers simply by their dress and stop them. The effectiveness of community governance is thus greatly enhanced by the enclosed spatial features of residential compounds.

The new institution of the 'community' takes charge of a wide range of functions. Bray (2008) vividly described how two communities in Wuhan quickly mobilized their residents during the SARS crisis in 2003. The community staff first posted flyers on all notice boards with information on SARS prevention measures. Then they mobilized volunteers – most of whom were Communist Party members – to conduct home visits to more than 1,800 families to identify any possible cases of infection. Any people with even the slightest signs of infection, such as higher-than-normal body temperature, were quarantined in their apartments and not allowed to be in contact with other residents. The community leaders also monitored movements into and out of their neighborhood.

In another case study in Guangzhou, Boland and Zhu (2012) described the new "green community" initiatives being implemented in dozens of cities. The green initiatives aim to reduce the ecological footprint of cities and improve the neighborhood environment by engaging public participation in sustainable consumption practices. Boland and Zhu observed that community leaders played a key role in the everyday implementation of the green initiatives, and that they worked closely with property-management companies to organize environment-themed cultural events and festivals. As the district governments assess "participation" primarily according to the number and size of these "green" events, in order to increase the headcounts, community staff would ask employees of private property-management companies in charge of individual *xiaoqu* to be present at the events. These case studies show that the community has matured as a neighborhood-level institution. In emergency situations such as the SARS epidemic and during major national events and campaigns, the community can work closely with private property-management companies and effectively mobilize residents to meet the goals set up by their administrative superiors, such as district and city governments.

Homeowners' associations

Currently, the community is one of the three major governance institutions at the neighborhood level, the other two being homeowners' associations and private property-management companies. In response to the increasing conflicts between developers and homeowners, in 2003 the government passed the *Regulations on Housing Property Management*, which provided a legal basis to allow self-organizing among homeowners to protect their rights. In reality, many homeowners' associations are weak and the selection of homeowners' representatives is often influenced by the community administration and by private developers (Read, 2003). Property-management companies cannot be relied on to protect homeowners' rights because many of them are subsidiaries of developers. When rights violations occur – for instance, when developers break contracts and construct extra buildings in the public green space – homeowners have to organize themselves independently to fight the developers.

Past studies have found that Chinese middle-class homeowners are modest in their protests and limited in their capacity to mobilize disruptive action (Cai, 2005). Most such mobilizations do not challenge the state authority but focus on protecting the neighborhood amenities and strictly adopt the official discourse of homeowners' rights. In 2008, residents in Shanghai organized a protest against the extension of the Maglev train (i.e., the bullet train connecting Pudong International Airport to the central city) to pass near their neighborhood, raising concerns over pollution, safety, and noise. The residents called their act a "stroll" instead of a protest, and it was referred to in the media as "harmony stroll" (*hexie sanbu*), echoing the government slogan of building a "harmonious society" (Wasserstrom, 2009).

Urban governance at the neighborhood scale has been restructured with the new institution of the community, the formation of home-owners' associations, and the ubiquity of private property-management companies. Community building in China is viewed by some as a neoliberal strategy by the government to fill the void in social service provision left by the retreat of the welfare state through self-governance – defined not as autonomy or equal rights to govern, but simply as managing one's own affairs within the parameters set up by the government (Bray, 2008). However, to what extent the new community institution in urban China can be characterized as neoliberal is still open to debate. As shown in the case studies on SARS prevention and environmental campaigns, many of the strategies adopted by the new community administration exhibit clear legacies from mass mobilizations of the socialist era. The community should be seen as the reinvention and adaptation of the previous socio-spatial governance institutions at the neighborhood scale.

CONCLUSIONS

Chinese cities are embedded in a complex system of hierarchical and horizontal authorities. This chapter has examined how decision-making power has shifted from central ministries to territorial authorities, especially to municipal governments, which now have substantial power in the development of land, housing, and infrastructure. The territorialization of the state, however, should not be understood as simply a one-way devolution of power from central authorities to local governments. As shown in the cases of the land, housing, and infrastructure sectors, both central authorities and municipal governments have enhanced their capacity to govern in the reform era. Driven by different priorities, central and local governments often clash in policymaking and implementation. Decentralization of power is accompanied by competition between central and local authorities, as seen in the attempts by the central government to assert control through regulations and the strategies of local officials to resist such regulations in favor of promoting growth within their localities. The chapter has also discussed the decline of former socialist institutions such as *danwei* and *hukou,* and the emergence of new institutions such as the community. These institutions will enmesh Chinese cities in a new power matrix.

The current system of urban governance faces a number of major issues. First, the power of local governments, greatly enhanced in the process of competitive decentralization, will have to be checked, and institutions that can do so effectively do not currently exist. In a nonelectoral political system such as China's, local officials are not accountable to residents and their policies are largely driven by GDP growth and career concerns. Effective institutions that allow public participation in policymaking are desperately needed to make local governments more accountable. Second, cities are vertically connected to upper-level governments, and there has been a lack of horizontal alliances among them. Inter-city networking needs to be fostered to promote cooperation and prevent race-to-the-bottom competition. Third, and most importantly, cities should be planned and built for people, not for profit (Brenner, Marcuse, and Mayer 2011). An alternative model of urban planning and policymaking is needed to reverse the current trend of cities becoming profit-making machines for local governments and private investors, and to make them instead into places for better living.

| 3 | Landscape

In the early 1990s, the city of Shanghai invited four prestigious international design firms to draft a master plan for Pudong New District, a large stretch of land on the east side of the Huangpu River. The site was selected by the central government to be developed into China's financial hub. After a decade of massive investment and construction, by the mid-2000s, Pudong had already acquired the look of a financial center, with dozens of sleek skyscrapers overlooking the historical Bund. The futuristic landscape of Pudong was chosen as a setting for the Hollywood film *Mission Impossible III* (2006), in which actor Tom Cruise jumped between the Bank of China building and the Oriental Pearl Tower, and a helicopter chase took place at night between the lit-up ultra-modern skyscrapers. The vertical skyline of Pudong is probably the most iconic urban landscape in China, symbolizing the transformation of the country and the status of Shanghai as China's financial center.

Compared to its counterparts in the West and in other developing countries, the Chinese state has enormous power and resources to undertake ambitious mega-projects to remake the urban landscape (Campanella, 2008; Ren, 2011). This chapter shifts the analysis from governance to the urban landscape and examines the planning, construction, and contestation of actual places typically observed in Chinese cities today, such as Central Business Districts, eco-cities, historical preservation zones, artist quarters, new architectural icons, and the kaleidoscope of settlement types on the urban periphery. Place-making is often a messy process, involving a multitude of actors such as government officials, planners, architects, developers, the media, and residents. Using case studies of particular buildings, streets, neighborhoods, and urban districts in Beijing, Shanghai, and Shenzhen, this chapter examines how places are planned, built, upgraded, branded, reinvented, used, and contested by different actors. The restless landscape offers a social text in which to read the power dynamics among the local and global actors in the place-making process, and it shows that Chinese cities have become wedded more closely than ever before to the larger global economy. We will begin with an introduction of the role of urban planning in engineering changes in the landscape.

THE THIRD SPRING OF URBAN PLANNING

With rapid urban development since 1990, the profession of urban planning in China has regained prominence and entered a "third spring" (Leaf and Hou, 2006). The first "spring" was in the 1950s, when the new socialist government initiated many large industrial projects and called on urban planners to help with economic planning and national industrialization. During the socialist years, urban planning played a subordinate role to economic planning, as cities were defined as the bases for industrialization, and construction of housing and infrastructure was purposely suppressed. The socialist urban planning was centered on a two-tiered system of making city master plans and detailed construction plans. It was implemented in a top-down manner with strong administrative intervention, heavy reliance on work units for implementation, and very little public participation (Wu, 2007). The "second spring" came in the period after the Cultural Revolution, when planners and architects were allowed to resume their work after a decade-long suspension. But real-estate activities in the 1980s progressed at a slow pace, and the role of planning in urban construction did not become immediately evident after its rehabilitation. The "third spring" is the period of massive urban renewal and redevelopment since 1990. Urban planning has now become a critical instrument for boosting the competitiveness of cities and enabling economic growth.

Both continuities and ruptures can be observed in the practices of urban planning in China today in comparison with those of the socialist period. First, urban planning today is still very much dominated by administrative orders from local governments and involves little participation by the public. The 1989 City Planning Act, for example, required all projects to apply for permission from municipal planning authorities, but the approval rights rest solely in the hands of the municipal officials and no public input is required. Relatedly, urban planning in China emphasizes design and construction that enable physical change in the built environment, to the exclusion of other modes of planning that protect public interests, such as regulation, advocacy, and community building (Abramson, 2007). Moreover, certain planning approaches, such as cellular design, have continued from the socialist period through today, as seen in the examples of *danwei* compounds in the pre-reform era and commodity housing estates (*xiaoqu*) in the post-reform era (Miao, 2003).

While bearing these continuities, urban planning today has also evolved to become a strategic instrument for building competitiveness and enabling economic growth, which was not the case in the socialist years. For example, "city strategic plans" are widely used to articulate the vision of government officials for future urban growth (Wu, 2007). In such plans, city governments and their planning bureaus identify various growth poles, belts, and zones, and propose residential new towns, university towns, high-tech parks, and other special economic development zones. Although such strategic plans are not legal documents and are not recognized by the Ministry of Construction, they are nevertheless widely used by city governments to demonstrate their ambitions, to attract attention from investors, and to legitimize land acquisition and housing demolition. Because of its instrumental character, urban planning in China tends to focus on large-scale redevelopment projects rather than small-scale neighborhood upgrading (Abramson, 2007). One of the consequences of this tendency is a gap in terms of living conditions between the officially planned and redeveloped zones and the leftover areas that have organically grown and are untouched by formal planning, such as old inner-city neighborhoods and migrant villages on the periphery that suffer from high density and inadequate infrastructure.

UBIQUITOUS CBDS

It is not an overstatement to say that almost every Chinese city dreams of having a Central Business District, if it doesn't have one already. Traditionally, Chinese cities were seats of administration, and allocating central city land specifically for business and commerce was an alien idea. When the concept of Central Business Districts (CBDs) was borrowed from the West in the early 1990s, however, local governments welcomed the idea with great enthusiasm, viewing it as a cure-all solution to remake the morbid built environment inherited from the socialist years. Shanghai and Beijing first built their CBDs in the 1990s, and, following suit, many other cities announced plans to build their own CBDs (Gaubatz, 2005). In 2003, the Ministry of Construction commissioned a survey to find out how many cities were planning to build a CBD, and the result was a staggering 36.[1] These included not only large cities with a strong economic base, such as Chongqing, Tianjin, Shenyang, Ji'nan, Zhengzhou, Xi'an, Chengdu, Wuhan, Nanjing, Hangzhou, Dalian, Ningbo, and Shenzhen, but also county-level cities without either the capacity or the need to have a CBD, such as Xiangyang and Huangshi (Hubei province), Wuxi and Shaoxing

(Jiangsu), Huainan (Anhui), Wenzhou (Zhejiang), Jinjiang (Fujian), Yiwu (Zhejiang), and Foshan (Guangdong). Now let's take a look at how Beijing built its CBD.

The plan of building a CBD in Beijing was first proposed in the *Beijing General City Plan*, which was approved by the State Council in 1993. In 1998, the Beijing city government issued the *Specific Controlling Plan of Beijing*, directing that the CBD be located in Chaoyang district. The Central Business District Administration Committee was established to supervise the overall development activities. The area allocated for the CBD was approximately 4 square kilometers at the crossing of the East Third Ring Road and Jian'guomenwai Avenue, a site that used to be an industrial area with a number of large manufacturing facilities. Members of approximately 54,000 households worked and lived in the area. But the city government envisioned a new modern business district emerging from there that could integrate business, exhibition, hotel, residence, and entertainment functions, and that would become a new headquarters and management center for financial, insurance, telecom, and information companies. To turn this zone of old state factories and run-down residential neighborhoods into a state-of-the-art CBD, the existing manufacturing facilities had to be relocated elsewhere, old residential buildings had to be demolished, and the residents had to be relocated (Ren, 2008a).

The first step to turn the area into a modern business district was to draft a master plan accommodating global business functions. Beijing followed Shanghai's practice of inviting international architectural design firms to prepare the master plan. In 2000, with the help of the Beijing Municipal Institute of City Planning and Design (BMICPD), the Chaoyang district government organized an initial design competition, inviting eight international firms to submit master-plan proposals. Among them were firms from the US, Germany, Japan, and Holland. The participation of international design firms was widely publicized in the media. To reflect the "international" nature of the design process for the CBD, the organizers also put together a jury committee composed of not only Chinese but also international experts in architecture and planning. The committee selected the design by Johnson Fain & Partners, a firm based in Los Angeles, for the first prize. In 2003, a second international design competition was held to select a detailed plan for a smaller core area of the CBD. The design proposal from Pei Cobb Freed & Partners, also from the US, took first place (Ren, 2008a).

Similar to what happened in the Pudong district of Shanghai, neither of the winning designs from the two competitions was actually used in intact form. Instead, state design institutes improvised a master plan in the midst of breakneck construction. In Chaoyang, Beijing Planning and Design Institute combined features from different design proposals to create the final master plan. For the local government, it mattered less that the original design proposals were abandoned, and that the new master plan from the design institute itself would probably not be strictly followed. What mattered more was that the final master plan resulted from "international" design competitions and therefore was a "global" product. The gesture of soliciting ideas from international architecture and planning firms was largely symbolic, and their participation in the design competitions was seen as a great success in itself, a marketing tool to promote the new CBD. The CBD was used as a display window to highlight Beijing's modernization and progress.

After more than two decades of development, Shanghai's and Beijing's CBDs have attracted a large number of foreign business firms and become major financial centers in the country. But compared to Beijing and Shanghai, other cities have not fared well in their rush to build. As early as the 1990s, Guangzhou was planning to build a CBD over a short period of 5–10 years in a designated area named Pearl River New Town, with ambitious ideas such as building dozens of office skyscrapers, a beach recreation area on the riverbank, municipal libraries, museums, and a signature opera house designed by Zaha Hadid. Two decades have passed and Pearl River New Town has yet to become a vibrant modern business district like Pudong in Shanghai or Chaoyang CBD in Beijing. The grand opera house has already been completed, but due to the haste with which it was constructed – the building had to be finished before the opening of the Asian Games in 2010 – the quality was largely compromised. The Chinese and English signs on the opera house were already beginning to peel off less than a year after its completion. As the case of Guangzhou and many other unfinished CBDs show, the Beijing and Shanghai model of making CBDs is unique, requiring strong policy incentives and massive capital infusion, and, therefore, it cannot and should not be imitated everywhere.

ART SPACE

Arts districts housing cultural and creative industries have also become a semi-permanent feature of the contemporary landscape of Chinese cities. In Beijing alone, there are more than a dozen artist colonies utilizing spaces in former factories and rural villages (Ren and Sun, 2012). In Shanghai, old factories, shipyards, and textile mills have been turned into cultural and creative industry parks with government subsidies (Wang, 2009; Zheng, 2010). The emergence of these arts districts is a result of the booming contemporary Chinese art scene and government policies to promote cultural and creative industries. The fate of the arts districts is, however, far from certain, since they are under constant pressure from real-estate development and hyper-gentrification. The 798 Factory is a case in point.

The 798 Factory is the first organically developed arts district in Beijing. Emerging in the 1990s, 798 opened up space that was badly needed for art exhibitions and festivals in the city, and made contemporary art accessible to the public. Throughout the 1980s and 1990s, the development of contemporary Chinese art was severely constrained by the lack of exhibition space (Angremy, 2008). Artists held shows in their private apartments and other temporary spaces to which the public had no access. The emergence of 798 as a cluster of studios and galleries changed this situation and provided an open platform for artists to interact with the public. The 798 Factory was originally part of a large radio electronic component factory built in the 1950s with the help of East German architects and engineers. The Chinese government poured subsidies into the construction of dozens of Bauhaus-style factory workshops. Similar to other state-owned enterprises, 798 Factory went through painful restructuring in the late 1990s. Factory workshops were shut down and workers were laid off with their salaries unpaid. The factory was eager to rent out workshop space on short-term leases and use the rent to cover its economic loss. A few artists moved into 798 in the late 1990s, attracted by its Bauhaus-style workshops and cheap rent. Word quickly spread in the art community in Beijing, and more artists followed suit, renovating the space to suit their needs. By 2004, 798 Factory had already become a dynamic artist quarter with a wide spectrum of institutions necessary for the development of contemporary art, such as galleries, exhibition spaces, artists' studios, independent bookstores, restaurants, offices, and coffee shops, all of which are located within the 1 square kilometer area of the factory compound (Ren, 2009).

In spite of the instant success of 798, its landlord repeatedly tried to evict artists and tear down factory workshops for redevelopment. The landlord that rented out space to artists was Seven Stars Group, a state-owned electronics factory that had planned to turn the area into part of Zhongguancun Electronics Park by 2005 and to redevelop the rest of the land into high-rise apartments. Despite protests by artists, in August 2004 Seven Stars demolished a large area of Bauhaus buildings near the south entrance of 798 and refused to renew artists' leases. Seven Stars threatened to close down the inaugural Dashanzi

International Art Festival, and artists mobilized the media, solicited support from foreign embassies in Beijing, and finally succeeded in pushing through the festival (Ye, 2008). In 2005, the artists decided to lobby the city government to turn 798 into an official arts district and, by doing so, to save it from demolition. Sculptor and Tsinghua University art professor Li Xiangqun, also a member of the People's Congress in Beijing, submitted a proposal to the Congress calling for the preservation of 798. After a few visits by city and district officials in 2006, the city government announced plans to preserve the area and turn it into one of Beijing's creative-industry clusters. A management office was set up, composed of members of the Chaoyang District Office of Development and Reform, the Propaganda Department, and the Bureau of Tourism.

The designation of 798 as an official arts district has been a double-edged sword – it saved the area from demolition, but it also meant that the government would take control of the district from then on. The government designation brought about a rapid reshuffling of tenants in 798. Several large international galleries and multinational corporations moved in, and the original artists moved out due to a sharp increase in rents. The trajectory of 798 is typical among arts districts in Chinese cities, where organic artist colonies go through a fast cycle of hyper-gentrification driven by both market forces and government policies for promoting cultural industries. By the time of the Beijing Olympics in 2008, the profile of 798 had already completely changed from an artist colony into an upscale arts district complete with prominent galleries, art shops, and restaurants catering to the tourist traffic. As 798 becomes a destination for urban tourism, creativity has moved elsewhere, to other arts quarters on the urban periphery with cheaper rents and more available studio space. Across the country, 798-style arts districts have appeared in other cities as well, such as Shenzhen, Chongqing, Chengdu, and Dalian, and arts districts/tourist quarters have become a fixed feature of the Chinese urban landscape.

HERITAGE SPACE

Historical buildings and neighborhoods often stand in the way when Chinese cities reinvent themselves as centres of finance, media, and cultural industry. A large number of historical buildings have vanished under the bulldozers since the urban renewal of the 1990s. Recently, recognizing the historical, but also the commercial, value of old buildings, city governments have passed preservation regulations and encircled large areas as preservation zones. The heightened awareness of historical preservation and the conflicting drive for development have combined to produce a particular type of heritage space where historical architecture is partially preserved and, in some cases, deliberately destroyed and then reconstructed, for the purpose of city-branding and to promote urban tourism (Ren, 2008b). The tension between preservation and development is felt most in ancient capital cities such as Beijing, Nanjing, and Xi'an.

Beijing experienced vast destruction in the second half of the twentieth century. In the 1950s, architect Liang Sicheng proposed to the government to build a new capital outside the old city of Beijing in order to avoid damaging the then well-preserved urban street networks, courtyard houses, and *hutongs* – narrow alleyways formed between rows of courtyard houses. Liang pointed out that Beijing was not planned and built for modern economic and transportation functions, and pushing forward industrialization in this old city would not only destroy the urban fabric, but also hinder the development itself (Wang, 2003). But Mao Zedong did not follow Liang's recommendations, envisioning instead a socialist industrial city built on top of ancient Beijing. Beijing rapidly industrialized in the 1950s, with more than 500 factories and enterprises constructed in the city. The old city wall, which had survived invasions, rebellions, and revolutions over hundreds of years, was demolished in 1958 by order of the central government.

The destruction of historical structures in Beijing continued with various urban renewal projects in the reform era. In an attempt at preservation, the city government passed a number of regulations to restrict building heights in the 1980s, and identified 33 historical protection zones in the 1990s, which constituted 29 percent of the old city. It also passed new laws guiding market transactions of courtyard houses, with the aim of guaranteeing private property ownership and thus giving owner-occupiers incentives to rehabilitate their courtyard houses. However, most of these measures have been ineffective, and Beijing's *hutong* neighborhoods have been disappearing at a faster rate than ever. In 1949, there were about 6,074 *hutongs* in Beijing; in 2005, the number had shrunk to 1,571.[2] Among those remaining, 671 are within the designated protection zones, while about 900 are outside them. Demolition has taken place on a massive scale both outside and inside the protection zones. Private developers have sometimes been able to tear down landmarked buildings if they obtained the land and demolition permits before the designation of the preservation zones. In 2012, ironically, the former residence in Dongcheng district of Liang Sicheng and his wife Lin Huiyin – two pioneers in the documentation and preservation of traditional Chinese architecture – was demolished, in spite of the fact that the Bureau of Cultural Relics had marked the house for preservation.[3] The overheated real-estate market and sky-rocketing property prices have made the enforcement of zoning laws difficult and placed preservation low on the agenda of the city government, and many developers are willing to pay the fine for demolishing landmarked buildings. Ranging between 50,000 and 500,000 RMB, the fine is a small price to pay compared to the enormous profits generated by redevelopment.

In addition to demolitions, a large number of historical structures have also fallen victim to various "preservation" projects in which old, authentic buildings are deliberately destroyed and replaced by fake historical buildings. Qianmen Avenue, where new gray-brick constructions replaced old *hutongs*, is one such case. Qianmen is in the geo-graphic center of the city, within walking distance of Tian'anmen Square. Historically, it is the front gateway connecting the Outer City and Inner City of imperial Beijing. During the Qing period (1644–1911), Qianmen was a booming marketplace, with a great congestion of merchants, shopkeepers, peasants, and laborers (Naquin, 2000). By the 1990s, Qianmen had become a run-down city quarter with dilapidated housing and densely populated *hutongs*, many of which lacked electricity, running water, and sewage. But it was a vibrant mixed-use neighborhood and known for the famous Dazhalan, an open-air street market selling cheap clothing, watches, pirated DVDs, and tourist souvenirs. The historical importance of Qianmen, its geographical proximity to Tian'anmen Square, and its high population density all made the rehabilitation of the area a challenging task. Qianmen remained one of the last areas in Beijing untouched by developers until the 2008 Olympics.

The Municipal Planning Bureau decided that the Qianmen area, with its crowded housing and chaotic street markets, needed to be made more presentable for the Olympics since the area was on the Olympic marathon route. As part of the city's pre-Olympic beautification program, a master plan was drafted to widen the narrow streets in the area, rebuild "authentic and historical" shop fronts, and displace street vendors and residents to alleviate the density problem. Ben Wood, an American architect who worked on the renovation of Faneuil Hall Marketplace in Boston, was invited to be the chief architect for the Qianmen Avenue renovations. Wood's name is well known in the architecture and real-estate circles in China for the Xintiandi project he supervised in Shanghai. By renovating a dozen residential-row houses built in the colonial era, Wood turned Xintiandi from a run-down inner-city neighborhood into the priciest property in Shanghai (Ren, 2008b). The new Qianmen Avenue followed the same formula as Xintiandi: private developers invest in renovating a "historical street" to raise property values, and later demolish and redevelop the larger area to reap higher profits. The new Qianmen Avenue is a great disappointment to Beijing's preservationists – yet another property redevelopment scheme in the guise of preservation. Nothing has been preserved here – all the gray-brick "historical" buildings are new constructions, rented to domestic and international companies such as ZARA, H&M, Quanjude (a known brand for Peking duck) and Ruifuxiang (specializing in silk and fabrics). The Qianmen project is the latest example of redevelopment in the name of "preservation," and across the country many similar projects, where new "heritage" space is created for place promotion and tourism, can be found in ancient cities such as Xi'an, Nanjing, Chengdu, Luoyang, and Hangzhou.

NEW ARCHITECTURAL ICONS

The contemporary Chinese urban landscape is dotted with new architectural icons, high-profile buildings commissioned to international architects by the state and the private sector as tools for place promotion, or as a way for individual politicians to leave a personal landmark to show their accomplishments. Beginning with the National Theatre in Beijing in 1998, designed by French architect Paul Andreu during Jiang Zemin's term as President, the central and local governments have repeatedly turned to prominent international architects to design their grand projects throughout recent years.

The National Stadium is among the most spectacular architectural monuments in the new Beijing. With 80,000 permanent spectator seats and another 11,000 temporary seats, the National Stadium is the central stage where the opening and closing ceremonies of the 2008 Olympics took place. The locals call the stadium the "bird's nest," as its grid-like steel structures resemble interwoven twigs. The choice of two prominent international architects – Jacques Herzog and Pierre de

Meuron, the laureates of the 2001 Pritzker Architecture Prize – reveals the ambition of government officials in China to demonstrate the country's rise as an eminent economic and political power on the world stage (Ren, 2008c).

For Herzog and de Meuron, two architects based in Basel, Switzerland, China was unfamiliar terrain. Herzog and de Meuron's decision to enter China was triggered by Rem Koolhaas's winning of the CCTV (Chinese Central Television) building project in Beijing in 2002. Herzog and de Meuron were also invited to the CCTV competition. However, they decided not to compete after learning about the poor protection of intellectual property rights and the unfair practices of design competitions in China. In winter 2002, they received the news that Rem Koolhaas – their friend and rival – had won the competition. They regretted the lost opportunity and believed that if they had participated, they would have won.[4] They sought advice from Uli Sigg, the former Swiss ambassador to China and a Chinese art collector. Uli Sigg recommended Ai Weiwei to be their local consultant. Ai Weiwei is a well-established artist who returned to Beijing after a 10-year stay in New York in the 1980s. As the son of China's famous poet of the 1920s, Ai Qing, Ai Weiwei had sufficient political capital to help Herzog and de Meuron navigate the complicated bureaucratic procedures and unpredictable domestic politics. Ai Weiwei first found a local design partner for Herzog and de Meuron – China Architecture and Design Group – with whom they could form a design consortium. He also turned out to be the most outspoken advocate for Herzog and de Meuron's design, when the project was later caught up in a cultural war between liberals and conservatives.

Many of the state-sponsored architectural mega-projects commissioned to international architects have led to heated debates in the local architectural community. Conservatives see the appointment of international – i.e., non-Chinese – architects to design these highest-profile national projects as a lost opportunity for Chinese architects, while liberals argue that international design competitions are imperative in order to integrate the Chinese architectural scene into the world (Ren, 2008c). In the case of the National Stadium, a number of engineers from the Chinese Academy of Sciences submitted a petition letter to Prime Minister Wen Jiabao, criticizing the extravagance and costs of the stadium. The central government responded to the petition and temporarily halted the construction in 2004, asking the architects to revise their design in order to cut costs. The government's decision soon became the focus of criticism by local cultural liberals who questioned the "system," namely, the inconsistent and non-transparent decision-making process of the authoritarian state. Ai Weiwei, for example, questioned the government's act of cutting the costs of Olympic projects in order to gain popular support, and he openly criticized the closed-door decision-making over the Stadium budget. The liberal cultural elites believe that China cannot make progress without opening up. Economic reforms have to be accompanied by the reform of the political system. Global competition and influences – both within architecture and beyond – can change China's way of doing politics, and redistribute power from the top to the people.[5]

Chinese cities have offered unprecedented opportunities for architects to see their dream projects built, but they might not be the places for the best architectural work to be done. The speed and scale of construction, the unchecked state power, and the lack of public participation have produced conditions ripe for the making of architectural icons, but do not leave any space, or time, for critical thinking, reflection, and engagement with the local urban context. Since the summer Olympics ended, most stadiums in Beijing's Olympic Park have been lying idle. The Bird's Nest is empty most of the time, charging tourists about 50 RMB for a visit inside, and the Water Cube (National Swimming Center) – which once housed the fastest pool in the world – has been turned into a water theme park.

XIAOQU

Between skyscrapers and heritage space, new architectural icons and artist quarters, one can find the housing estates – called *xiaoqu* in Chinese (meaning "small quarters") – where most urban Chinese live, young and old, rich and poor. *Xiaoqu* vary in regard to their size, the ownership of housing units, the age of construction, and the socio-economic status of their residents. Older *xiaoqu* are the remaining former *danwei* housing compounds, and, in most of these cases, the sitting tenants have already purchased the apartments that they used to rent at a minimal cost. In these older *xiaoqu*, there are often denser webs of neighborhood-based ties, as residents have known each other over longer periods of time and through the *danwei* connection. The newer *xiaoqu* are mostly commodity-housing projects built after 1990 by either private developers or municipal governments and, in these newer ones, residents know each other less well and neighborhood-based networks are less developed. Large *xiaoqu* often comprise tens of thousands of households, and even smaller ones can have a dozen high-rise or mid-rise apartment buildings housing several hundred families. In spite of the variations, Chinese *xiaoqu* share one common design feature: gating. Most *xiaoqu*, large and small, old and new, have physical walls, fences, and gates to mark their boundaries, although in many cases the gates are left open all the time, and some *xiaoqu* are only partially gated (Yip, 2012). In the many discussions of this design feature in the literature, urban China scholars have offered different, but complementary, interpretations of the origin and meaning of the practice of gating. For example, it is interpreted as an indication of the quest for safety and security (Miao, 2003), as a legacy of neighborhood collectivism from the socialist era (Huang, 2006), as a sign of the desire for privacy associated with private property ownership (Pow, 2009), and as a status symbol, in the case of exclusive high-end communities (Giroir, 2006; Wu, 2010a). Recent surveys in Shanghai and Guangzhou show that although gating may enhance residents' sense of safety and security, it may not necessarily contribute to community attachment. Researchers find that in general, in the commodity-housing *xiaoqu* built since the 1990s, social networks are weaker than in *danwei*-based neighborhoods, and the presence of physical gates does not help to build community cohesion (Yip, 2012; Li, Zhu, and Li 2012).

Although the effects of gating in preventing crimes and fostering community attachment are uncertain and can vary greatly from place to place, the enclosed or semi-enclosed spatial layout of *xiaoqu* significantly shapes residents' use of public space and everyday activity. In most *xiaoqu*, there is public green space – in smaller *xiaoqu*, it can be just a tiny park with a few benches, while in newer and wealthier ones, there are artificial lakes, waterfalls, bridges, and meticulously maintained lawns for residents to use. These green spaces have often become a magnet for neighborhood socializing and activities. The circular design of *xiaoqu* both brings benefits and presents problems. On the one hand, the gating shields a neighborhood from outside traffic and noise, and creates a quieter and more user-friendly public space for residents; on the other hand, it produces an urban fabric with a cellular structure and makes cities feel more inward-looking, lacking public life on the streets.

In the *xiaoqu* where my family lives in Harbin, the central public space becomes a busy theater exploding with activities every night. Residents come out from their private apartments to the park, to chat with neighbors, play chess, sing Peking opera and revolutionary songs, practice folk dances, and play Ping Pong, badminton, and basketball. Some residents just take a walk circling the small park, watching others singing, dancing, and playing. One round of the park probably takes no more than three to four minutes, and the walkers do 15 to 20 rounds, clockwise and counter-clockwise. A few times, out of curiosity, I joined the residents in their march around the park, wondering why they would not take an evening walk outside the *xiaoqu*. The answer became obvious after two to three rounds of walking – it was interesting to watch the other people, and it was much more enjoyable than walking along a busy street with narrow sidewalks and heavy traffic.

As most urban Chinese live in *xiaoqu*, they offer a crucial site to understand sociality, civility, and the meaning of public space. Chinese *xiaoqu* have been studied as a variation of "gated communities" and compared with gated communities in the West. But gating means and does very different things in China, such as creating a public space from within. "Gated communities" cannot capture the distinctiveness of the spatial design of and social life in a *xiaoqu*, which has to be understood in its own terms. Although not every *xiaoqu* is a beehive of neighborhood socializing and leisure activities, behind many gates, closed or semi-closed, manned or unmanned, one can find a small public space used to its full potential by residents. Most public space in China – space that can be accessed by anyone – is used by small groups sharing some form of common association, such as people living in the same neighborhood, which is a great departure from the meaning, form, and use of public space in the West.

THOUSAND-MILE CITIES: LANDSCAPE ON THE PERIPHERY

In the literature on urban China, scholars routinely use the term *suburbanization* to describe the sprawl of Chinese cities (Zhou and Ma, 2000; Feng and Zhou, 2003; Li and Tang, 2005). Surpassing "100-mile cities," a term coined by architecture critic Deyan Sudjic (1992) to describe American suburbanization, Chinese cities often extend their geographic jurisdiction over thousands of miles. The power imbalance between city governments and rural counties makes annexation of rural areas a routine exercise for urban authorities. The administrative jurisdiction of Shanghai, for example, covers more than

6,000 square kilometers (about 2,280 square miles). But, in spite of this administrative sprawl, suburbanization – a concept with strong North American connotations evoking images of lower-density, automobile-based residential settlements – is misleading when used to describe the outward expansion of Chinese cities. Urban peripheries of Chinese cities, the areas sandwiched between historical urban cores and the rural hinterland, are mosaics of different social worlds nothing like American suburbs. On the Chinese urban periphery, one can find residential new towns of massive scale, exclusive European-themed villas, migrant villages,[6] brand-new university campuses, military-style manufacturing facilities and workers' dorms, and often times, agricultural fields in the midst of urban construction as well. Heterogeneity of socio-economic composition, high population density, and dependency on public mass transit characterize the nature and process of urban territorial expansion. This section examines a number of settlement types typically found in the landscape of the Chinese urban periphery.

Satellite new towns

Since 2000, satellite new towns have begun to emerge on the outskirts of large Chinese cities. Some are master-planned and developed by city and district governments, but there are also many that have been developed by large real-estate companies such as Vanke and Gemdale. The development of large residential new towns is driven by a number of factors. First of all, large cities have been actively promoting the idea of developing satellite new towns at their peripheries in order to alleviate the population pressure in central city districts. Second, as housing prices in inner-city neighborhoods have risen out of reach for the majority of residents – both newcomers and established local residents – many families have settled in residential new towns on the periphery where they can afford to have a place of their own. Third, those who have been displaced by various urban renewal programs and mega-events have also moved to satellite new towns, where most resettlement housing is constructed. The new towns located closer to city centers are often more densely populated and better equipped with amenities. Drawn by the large population, international retail chains such as IKEA, Carrefour, and Walmart are ubiquitous in these neighborhoods. These communities have also become entry points for migrant workers, who often open up small neighborhood shops, filling the gaps left by large chain stores.

In recent years, a number of super-large residential new towns have emerged on the periphery of large cities, operating like cities in their own right. The largest residential new town to date, Tiantongyuan in north Beijing, currently has a population of 600,000. In the beginning phase of the development in the 1990s, residents complained about the inconvenience of the place – for instance, its lack of public transit, hospitals, and schools. The situation has improved gradually over the years, but the infrastructure still cannot catch up with the scale of the population growth. In 2005, Subway No.5 was extended to Tiantongyuan and brought some relief for residents, but the improved public transit connection also attracted more people to move into the new town. Most Chinese satellite new towns follow the cellular design of an enclosed *xiaoqu*, with walls and gates encircling the estate on four sides. *Xiaoqu* design might work better at a small scale, but when implemented for a community with tens of thousands of residents, it causes severe traffic congestion by separating the road networks within the new town from those outside. More and more middle-class families are beginning to own cars, with the result that every morning, the roads to the main gates in Tiantongyuan become a giant parking lot, choked with cars trying to get to the main streets outside.

In addition to densely populated new towns with inadequate infra-structure, there are also many other satellite new towns that have failed to attract residents. These are mostly places far away from city centers and not connected yet by commuter trains. The best-known empty new towns are the ones developed under the *One City-Nine Town* program in Shanghai. In 2001, nine towns in the larger Shanghai metropolitan area were chosen as sites for the development of residential, manufacturing, and commercial sub-centers. European planning firms were invited to draft urban master plans for these new towns with the idea that each one would adopt the built-environment features of a European country – for example, Anting would be a German town and Songjiang a British one. However, a decade after the start of the program, these themed new towns have attracted very few residents. The low-rise apartment buildings in Anting, master-planned and designed by German firm Albert Speer, remained mostly empty at my last visit in 2010. And the nearby "Thames Town" in Songjiang, with imitations of British-style buildings, is primarily a destination for young couples to take wedding photos.[7] These newly built residential neighborhoods are beyond the financial reach of local residents and displaced peasants, yet they are not attractive to middle-class Shanghai residents, owing to their lack of public transport. Developers, many of whom have strong connections with the government, have dropped out of the program because it fails to promise profitability, and the deficit from land acquisition, relocation of peasants, and new construction has skyrocketed for district governments. By 2010, a few of the original nine towns with weaker economies had already abandoned their development plans.

University towns

Since 2000, there has been a wave of construction of new university campuses on urban peripheries across the country. Some universities have sold their downtown campuses and transferred land-use rights to private developers in order to raise funds to construct new campuses far away from city centers. Cities such as Shenzhen, Guangzhou,

Nanjing, Changchun, and Shanghai have encircled large plots of agricultural land at the urban fringe for the construction of university towns. University towns are often created as a strategy to boost commercial real-estate development in remote areas by attracting a population of students and faculty first, providing a consumer base. Some well-publicized examples of such developments include, for example, Songjiang University Town in Shanghai, built between 2000 and 2005, located about 30 kilometers from the city center and occupying an area of 500 acres of former agricultural land; Nanjing University Town, composed of three smaller universities towns and developed in 2002, with a planned area of 80 square kilometers and aiming to attract a population of 230,000; and Guangzhou University Town, about 17 kilometers from the city center and covering an area of 40 square kilometers. As more and more schools relocate from inner cities to the periphery, many university towns have over time grown to be satellite new towns, each with a population of between 100,000 and 200,000.

University towns across the country follow similar patterns of development – land acquisition and property development by the state and public–private partnerships, and they exhibit similar problems too: poor public transport and a lack of cultural amenities. In the case of Songjiang University Town, land was acquired from farmers and the project was commissioned to a development company with strong connections to the Songjiang district government. The university town is poorly served by public transport. Prior to the opening of Subway No.9 in 2007, there were only four bus routes connecting the university town to the central city. Even with the opening of the new subway, students and professors still need to take a bus to reach the subway station, and the average commute to the city is more than an hour. It remains to be seen how many of China's university towns will truly become the centers of innovation that local governments claim them to be.

Exclusive villas

Exclusive villas on the periphery distinguish themselves from other middle-class housing estates by their low-density layout, family orientation, abundant green space, higher percentage of foreign expats, and the overall high socio-economic status of the residents. In the early stage of villa development, many exclusive residential properties targeted mainly foreign expats working for multinational companies. These expat enclaves have various amenities catering to their foreign residents, such as elite international schools, state-of-the-art gyms, and shopping facilities specializing in products from the home countries of the expats. But, over time, the clientele of exclusive villas has shifted to the Chinese nouveau riche. Many villa developments use the names of exotic foreign places, such as Orange County, French Riviera, Fifth Ave, and Long Beach, in order to appeal to wealthy Chinese desperately seeking status symbols and distinction. For their architecture, developers often liberally borrow design motifs from Europe and North America, and they also do not hesitate to mix architectural styles from different places and periods. For example, French chateaus and suburban American bungalows are often mixed with Chinese gardens with *fengshui* elements (Giroir, 2006). These communities of exclusive villas often have convenient access to expressways and airports, and can be easily reached by car, but most of them resist extensions of public transportation to their territories.

Manufacturing zones

The Chinese urban periphery is also a production space containing various industrial parks, export-processing zones, free-trade zones, and logistic hubs. Most industries have relocated from the center to the periphery, and city governments have been providing various incentives to attract foreign direct investment to these industrial zones. Mega-structures of modern factories and barracks-style workers' dorms dot the landscape of the production space, where the majority of the world's consumer products are manufactured and shipped with "Made in China" labels.[8] Due to a lack of alternative rental options, the majority of workers live in the dormitories provided by their employers within the factory compounds, or outside but within walking distance. Enterprises either purchase land from local governments to build their dormitories or rent dorms built by local governments and individuals to house their workers. In either case, managers can better control and monitor workers by keeping them in close range and concentrating them in the same space. Smith and Pun (2006) conducted a case study of a factory in Shenzhen, China Wonder Electronics, and they described the spatial layout of what they call the "dormitory labor regime."

> Empire-like, the dormitory compound (around 12,000 square meters) was like a housing estate, with four buildings for workers' accommodation and one building for housing managers. These five buildings were enclosed by a long wall and gated by a giant iron door. There was a small side door, open 24 hours and watched over by security guards. Walking through the side door and the security tower, there were two open areas for workers' recreational activities, such as playing badminton and basketball. There were a few tables and several dozen chairs at another corner where workers could chat. A shop was crowded with workers in the evening time, not buying daily necessities but watching TV programs. The shop was adjacent to two huge dining halls, which could each seat one thousand workers. (2006: 1463–4)

The spatial layout of the dormitory labor regime closely resembles *danwei* compounds of the socialist era, adopting the same cellular design by encircling working, living, and recreational space in the same quarter. Such living arrangements can certainly enable managers to better monitor their workers, but they also help to build solidarity among workers and facilitate mobilization when conflicts occur between workers and managers. Recently, there have been frequent incidents of walkouts and strikes by factory workers demanding higher wages, indicating the contentious labor relations on the periphery (Chan, 2011). Smith and Pun (2006) observed that leaders designated to negotiate with the management on behalf of workers were all elected in the dorms. Thus, the Chinese urban periphery is a strategic site for large-scale mobilization and social movements among the disenfranchised industrial working class.

From satellite new towns to university towns and factory-dorm complexes, the urban fringes of China's mega-cities are patchworks of heterogeneous land uses. These new settlements, exhibiting different landscape features, are produced by similar underlying logics of state-led capital accumulation. In almost every type of new development, the forces of state power decentralized to city and district governments – manifested in the acquisition of land, relocation of residents, commissioning of international architects, policing of marginalized populations, and implementation of favorable policies to lure foreign investment – can be clearly identified. Thousand-mile cities have begun to appear as city governments encircle more and more land, continue outward expansion, and authorize new developments on the periphery.

ECO-CITIES

Local Chinese officials have until recently tended to view economic growth and environmental protection as incompatible. With their own career advancement in mind, local officials have focused largely on boosting economic performance as measured by GDP growth, while environmental performance has languished at the bottom of policy agendas. Consequently, the Chinese economic miracle has been accompanied by a significant increase in environmental degradation and acute public health crises, as evidenced by numerous incidents of water and air pollution, skyrocketing levels of carbon emissions, energy-inefficient new buildings, the rapid loss of farmlands and forests, and the emergence of hundreds of so-called cancer villages.[9]

In response to the unfolding environmental crisis and growing popular discontent over environmental degradation, the Chinese government announced in 2005 that the nation's eleventh Five-Year Plan would follow a different model – shifting from "growth first" to "sustainable development."[10] In 2008, the Ministry of Environmental Protection (MEP) was established, and an impressive number of environmental laws, regulations, and policies have since been promulgated (Qi et al., 2008). At the local level, there has been intense competition for the National Model City for Environmental Protection (NMCEP) designation and a wave of construction of eco-cities.

The national government has experimented with a number of programs to incentivize local governments toward environmental protection. Enacted in 1997, the NMCEP incentive program was among the earliest. According to the MEP, by 2012 some 83 cities and districts in more than a dozen provinces had attained National Model City status, the majority of them located in the more developed coastal regions.[11] Specific criteria for becoming a National Model City include meeting a set of requirements for air and water quality as well as reducing emissions, as assessed through an initial site visit by MEP officials and annual follow-up visits after National Model City status is awarded. The whole evaluation process can take three to five years and requires collaboration among many different departments (Li, Miao, and Lang, 2011).

Recently, a more prestigious program, awarding the designation of "eco-city (*shengtai chengshi*)," has replaced NMCEP as the most desirable sustainability award for city governments. Similar designations, such as eco-provinces, eco-counties, eco-villages, and eco-districts, have proliferated. As of 2011, 14 Chinese provinces were striving to make themselves into eco-provinces, and more than 1,000 cities and counties had announced plans and timetables to achieve eco-city or eco-county status.[12] A separate program – certifying "eco-villages" – aims to promote sustainable urbanization of rural areas. Other incentive programs have been launched as well, such as the "low-carbon pilot program" in five provinces and eight cities, and the "new energy demonstration cities program," aiming to be active in 100 cities by 2015.[13] The competition for these awards is intense; Shenzhen has just boldly announced that it will become the first low-carbon city in the country.[14] At the neighborhood level, there has been the "green community" program that aims to raise public awareness of recycling, energy conservation, and sustainable living (Boland and Zhu, 2012). Local officials are compelled to pursue sustainability awards by peer pressure, career and reputational concerns, and the desire for place distinction.

As smaller cities compete for National Model City status, larger cities with more political clout and financial resources have begun building flagship eco-city projects. The largest eco-city projects are found in major urban regions, such as the Dongtan project in Shanghai (stalled since 2008), Tianjin Eco-city in Tianjin (under construction), and Caofeidian near Beijing (in the planning phase). These eco-city projects often involve an international network of consultants, planners, and sustainability experts, are financed by both local and foreign sources, and receive strong political support from central ministries as well as provincial and municipal governments. Eco-cities are intended to serve as role models for sustainable urban living in the future, by experimenting with cutting-edge environmental technologies and promoting harmony between humans and nature.

Tianjin Eco-City is a joint initiative between the Tianjin city government and the government of Singapore. The project is located about a one-hour drive from the city limits of Tianjin and covers an area of 30 square kilometers of wasteland that lacks fresh water. The goal, for the joint venture Sino-Singapore Tianjin Eco-City Investment and

Development Co. Ltd, is to turn the wasteland into a green community of 350,000 residents by 2020. According to the project's planners, upon completion, Tianjin Eco-City will possess many enviable features of sustainable urban living. For example, clean and renewable solar and geothermal energy will account for 20 percent of its total energy consumption. All buildings in the eco-city will meet international standards for green construction, and every structure will have insulation and double-glass windows to save energy. A light rail public transit system will be built, and 90 percent of the city's traffic will be either pedestrian or via bicycle or public transport. Existing biodiversity will be preserved, and lush green plants for residents' recreational use will replace the current saltpan. Water and waste will be meticulously recycled, and the new eco-city will also become a research and development center for environmental technologies, attracting clean-tech companies from Singapore. Lastly, to promote "social harmony," a mixed-income housing scheme will be introduced and the city government will subsidize low-income residents.[15] Since Tianjin Eco-City is still in its beginning phase, it is too early to tell whether these expensive green technologies and ambitious housing programs will be implemented and, if they are, what social and environmental benefits they will bring.

In a recent study, anthropologist Shannon May followed a flagship eco-village project in northeastern Liaoning province, where she observed the devastating consequences for communities of sustainability projects promoted by international experts and local governments. The China-US Center for Sustainable Development chose Huangbaiyu village as the site for an experiment in sustainable rural urbanization, and a group of international experts and local officials together drafted a master plan to redesign Huangbaiyu. The plan deemed indigenous housing construction and traditional resource-management systems backward and inefficient, and imposed new methods of construction and household management on villagers. But these changes required the relocation of all 400 families in the community, who also had to pay some of the new construction costs. Garden areas and grazing land were classified by the experts as wasteland and converted for cropping, which significantly distorted the local ecological system. May found that, by 2005, local families had become more impoverished than before the project began in 2003, as many of them had lost both their homes and their access to common resources, as well as having to pay for the new model-housing units built as part of the sustainability project (May, 2008).

Although most eco-city projects offer enticing blueprints for green urban living, they do not take into account the actual needs of residents and do not involve any public participation in the planning phase. Public consultation is universally missing from the various eco-city and eco-village projects. In the case of Huangbaiyu eco-village, local peasants wanted neither to move into new model housing nor to change their former ways of organizing village life – but they were given no choice to do otherwise. Tianjin Eco-City intends to attract 350,000 residents in the next 10 years, but it is unclear how the Sino-Singaporean consortium will convince people to relocate there without soliciting the perspectives of potential future residents. Other eco-city experiments with similar ambitions, such as Lingang New City in Shanghai, have to date attracted very few residents.[16]

The various green initiatives undertaken by the central and local governments are indicative of a new environmental turn in urban governance. Driven by the potential for economic upgrading and career advancement, local officials eagerly pursue National Model City status, build eco-city projects, and experiment with new policies geared toward improving environmental quality. Although all of these examples represent positive changes in state responses to environmental issues, the current green initiatives are invariably led by the central or local state in consultation with international experts, with little input from the public (Ren, 2012). The top-down nature of China's green programs presents new obstacles to building a sustainable urban future.

CONCLUSIONS

For both visitors and natives, the chaotic and fast-changing urban landscape in China can be overwhelming and hard to decipher. This chapter has explained why Chinese cities look the way they do by analyzing a number of ubiquitously observed settlement types. With examples of specific projects and places, it has shown how new places are made and old places are reinvented, as well as how these places are contested by a network of local and non-local actors who are staking claims to the new Chinese city. This survey of the restless Chinese urban landscape is intended to illustrate two points. First, the state plays a critical role in remaking Chinese cities through policies, master plans, sponsorship of international architects, partnerships with private capital, and repression of popular demands. Second, Chinese cities are deeply embedded in transnational flows of capital, information, and expertise, and they will be continually shaped by these forces. The interplay of Chinese state power and transnational flows of expertise can lead to unpredictable results, as in the cases of the numerous eco-city projects and iconic buildings. Eco-cities are experiments in building a greener urban future, but they are mostly collaborations between local governments and international planning firms, excluding the people from the decision-making process, and, as the case studies have shown, some of the sustainability projects have stalled because of policy changes or have driven local residents into deeper poverty. Iconic architectural monuments have drastically transformed the landscape of the Chinese city, but such new architectural icons often become subjects of criticism and contestation, and the legitimacy of the state is challenged as political elites remake Chinese cities for capital and recognition, instead of for people to live in.

4 | Migration ————————————————————

TRAVEL AT THE CHINESE NEW YEAR

The Chinese New Year, also called the Spring Festival, is the most important national holiday in the country. Every year between mid-January and early March, hundreds of millions of Chinese make the journey back home to reunite with their families and spend the holiday together. *Chunyun*, a Chinese word that literally means "spring transport," often invokes nightmarish images of the New Year traffic that paralyzes the national transit system year after year. In *chunyun* season, the entire country is on the move. Between January and March of 2010, more than 2.5 billion trips were made – a number almost double the national population – mostly by bus or by train.[1] A majority of *chunyun* travelers are rural migrant workers who have left farming behind and come to cities in search of a better life, and they go back home only once a year, during the New Year.

In the documentary film *Last Train Home* (2009), director Lixin Fan follows the journey of a migrant family traveling from a factory town in Guangdong back to its home town in Sichuan for the New Year. The family goes to the train station every day to check if tickets are available. The family members' anxiety escalates, as they still do not have tickets a week before New Year's Eve. They finally get hold of three tickets, pack their suitcases full of gifts, and head to Guangzhou train station – a major railway hub in the manufacturing zone in the south and a place known for the congestion of *chunyun* traffic made up of migrant workers. The trains are delayed due to bad weather, and the family joins tens of thousands of other migrant workers waiting for days at the train station, without knowing when their train will arrive. Finally, the train comes and there is a panic in the crowd. The family members are pushed and squeezed, and they get on the train exhausted. There is no place to lie down for the entire journey of more than 36 hours. The train passes through the vast mountainous terrain of western China. The mountain peaks covered with snow in Sichuan cast a sharp contrast with the industrial landscape in the Pearl River Delta. Looking outside the window, one passenger on the train says, "if the family couldn't spend the New Year together, life would be meaningless."

The rural-to-urban migration in China, involving more than 221 million people, is the largest-scale migration in human history. It is a story of hope and liberation, but also hardship, exploitation, and human suffering. Migrant workers in China are often referred to as "the floating population." According to the 2010 census, the number of people "floating" – officially defined as those living outside the place in which their *hukou* registration is recorded for more than six months – has exceeded 221 million, more than the total volume of international migration worldwide. This is an 83 percent increase since the 2000 census. From factories and construction sites to restaurants and massage parlors, migrant workers are often found in undesirable workplaces shunned by urbanites and have become the largest working class in cities. In spite of their large numbers, migrant workers in cities are often not very visible, as they work and live on the margins of urban glamor. Currently, the average income of migrant workers is only a third that of urban residents.[2] The huge gap in socio-economic status between migrants and urbanites, originating from and exacerbated by the *hukou* system, turns the 221 million migrant workers into second-class citizens in their own country.

The geographic pattern of migration reflects the uneven development of the country, as most migrants leave the poorer agricultural regions in the western interior for the more developed east coast and large urban centers. Although there are rural-to-rural moves and urban-to-urban moves, rural-to-urban moves – such as that of the Zhang family portrayed in the documentary – are the predominant modes of migration movement. Provinces in the central and western regions such as Sichuan, Guangxi, Hubei, and Hunan are the major sending areas, and large cities and provinces on the southeast coast are the main receiving areas. In the aftermath of the 2008 world economic recession, with factory closures in coastal regions and increased stimulus spending in western and central regions, more and more migrants from the western and central region began to look for work closer to their home towns rather than moving to the east coast.

There is a large and growing literature on China's internal migration, including studies on their adaptation to urban life, migrant children's education, and the impact of migration on the countryside that is left behind (Murphy, 2002; Tang and Yang, 2008; Liang, Guo and Duan, 2008; Lin, 2011). This chapter focuses on the nexus between migration and the transformation of Chinese cities and, specifically, it examines the housing and labor conditions of migrants in cities. Unlike in other mega-cities in the global South, in China one does not see many large-scale squatter settlements of self-built shelters on illegally occupied land. A majority of migrants in China are accommodated in factory dorms provided by employers, at the construction sites where they work, and in various migrant enclaves such as "Villages-in-the-City" (ViCs). This chapter takes a close look at ViCs, an informal type of migrant housing arrangement widely observed in China, especially in the south, where large migrant communities form in villages within and outside city limits as villagers rent out properties to migrant workers. City governments routinely raid or "redevelop" ViCs and displace migrants, but they do not offer alternative housing arrangements. At the workplace, the repetitive work, long working hours, and harsh treatment often push migrant workers to their limits. In 2010, 18 workers at Foxconn, a large electronics manufacturer, committed suicide in a month. Both inside factories and outside on the streets, labor protests and strikes erupt frequently in the factory belts in the south, where workers demand their unpaid wages and better treatment from both employers and local governments. Under pressure from the central government to maintain stability, local governments have become increasingly innovative in dealing with labor disputes. This chapter will discuss these recent trends in the working conditions of migrants, labor protests, the changing state responses, and the emerging sector of labor NGOs that help migrants to claim their rights in the city they inhabit.

HOUSING DISPARITY

The housing disparity between migrant workers and urbanites in China is unprecedented in the world. The housing reform that swept China beginning in the 1980s had created a staggering 72 percent homeownership rate among urban residents (i.e., those with local urban *hukou*) by 2010, but the reform did not take into account the housing needs of the large number of migrant workers. Homeownership among migrant workers in cities is still less than 1 percent. The jarring housing disparity between urbanites and migrant workers is due to both socio-economic gaps and the institutional barrier of *hukou*, and the two reinforce each other and perpetuate the disadvantaged position of migrants in the housing sector.

Based on migrant housing surveys conducted in Shanghai, Beijing, and Guangzhou between 1998 and 2005, urban planner Weiping Wu (2010b) reports that most migrants have very few housing choices, and they remain renters even after years of living in the city. Table 4.1 shows that, among the seven major types of urban housing, only two are available to migrant workers – commodity housing and private rentals. Commodity housing is available for anyone to purchase at market

Table 4.1: Housing types and availability for migrants in cities

	DESCRIPTION	MIGRANTS	URBANITES
Commodity housing (*shangpin fang*)	Available for anybody to purchase at market price	Yes	Yes
Private rental housing	Anybody can rent already-purchased commodity housing, municipal and work-unit housing (with permission), resettlement housing, and other types of private housing	Yes	Yes
Economic and Comfortable Housing (*jingji shiyong fang*)	Reserved for low- and medium-income urban families	No	Yes
Low-rent housing (*lianzu fang*)	Reserved for families with low income and/or a smaller living area per capita than local minimum standard	No	Yes
Municipal public housing	Sitting urban tenants can purchase ownership or use rights to their rental home from their municipality	No	Yes
Work-unit public housing	Sitting urban tenants can purchase ownership or use rights to their rental home from their work units	No	Yes
Resettlement Housing (*dongqian fang*)	Reserved for families being relocated for various redevelopment projects; prices are subsidized	No	Yes

Source: Adapted from Wu (2004) and Huang (2003).

prices; however, the very low income of migrants and skyrocketing housing prices put commodity housing far out of their reach. Local governments have different public-housing programs targeting low-income families, such as Economic and Comfortable Housing – subsidized housing for purchase – and Low-Rent Housing, that is, subsidized housing for rental, but only urban *hukou* holders may qualify for such programs. Other types of public housing, such as work units, municipal housing, and resettlement housing, are available for purchase at subsidized prices only for urban *hukou* holders. Since 2010, there have been affordable housing programs for migrants without local *hukou*, but the effects of these programs are still unclear. Many of the new affordable housing units are built on the urban fringe and migrant workers find them less attractive, as they prefer living closer to work. In the end, what are left for migrants are private rentals, and due to their low income, migrants often rent units in poor condition and in less desirable locations. Wu (2010b) notes that migrants have little incentive to improve their rental shelters, and the housing conditions of migrants are much worse than those of their urban counterparts.

VILLAGES-IN-THE-CITY (VICS)

Many migrant workers, except those for whom temporary housing arrangements are provided by their employers, look for a place to live on their own in the private rental market – for example, renting a place in work-unit housing quarters or from farmers who build property on their allocated residential land. The latter practice has become a major housing solution for migrant workers, especially in cities in the Pearl River Delta. Such pockets of migrant living are called *chengzhongcun* in Chinese, which literally means "Villages-in-the-City" (ViCs).[3] The definition of ViCs remains fuzzy today, as the scale, land-use features, land ownership, and relations with city government vary from village to village. But, for our purposes in discussing migrant housing, it suffices to define ViCs as residential quarters created in former villages both within and outside city limits as farmers build rental properties to cater to the housing demands of migrant workers. In the Pearl River Delta, village organizations often have a stronger capacity to mobilize resources for property development, and urban governments generally have a weaker hand in regulating construction activities on rural land. Large cities in the Pearl River Delta, such as Shenzhen and Guangzhou, have seen the development of hundreds of ViCs that provide affordable housing for millions of migrant workers.

Large volumes of migrant inflows and a limited supply of affordable housing for migrants make conditions ripe for the formation of ViCs. But the fact that migrant enclaves have not appeared in work-unit compounds or any other type of urban neighborhoods, but rather in villages that were (and in some cases still are) on the urban fringe, has to be explained by China's unique two-tier administrative system divided between city governments and rural authorities, such as county, town, and village governments. As rural land is collectively owned, peasants have the right to build housing on their allocated residential land. As millions of migrants come to cities, farmers seize the opportunity to build properties and rent rooms to them. In terms of regulation and infrastructure provision, municipal planning authorities do not intervene in construction activities initiated by peasants because their jurisdiction only covers state-owned land. City authorities also avoid rural areas when building infrastructure, so that there is a sharp difference in public infrastructure across the boundaries between areas under jurisdiction of city authorities and those under rural authorities. This unique configuration of separate land ownership and administrative systems has thus given rise to ViCs.

Geographically, ViCs are located both within and outside city limits. Those centrally located are often older and more developed, with village landlords who have better connections with city governments, while those on the far edge are newer developments with fewer government connections and often find themselves hit harder by government campaigns to "urbanize" or "redevelop" ViCs.

The demographic composition in ViCs has become more diverse over the years. In the 1990s, ViCs were mostly composed of migrants from the same region, such as Zhejiang village in Beijing, where most migrants were from Zhejiang province, and they heavily relied on family, relative, and lineage networks (e.g., members with the same last name and from the same village) for mutual help and to survive in the city (Zhang, 2002). Nowadays, migrant residents in ViCs are more diverse and come from all corners of the country. In a study on Guangzhou, Zhang (2005) reported that in Ruibao village, located about 1 mile from downtown, 2,000 indigenous villagers rented rooms to more than 60,000 migrants from Sichuan, Hunan, Guangxi, and other provinces, speaking a variety of dialects. ViCs are attractive housing solutions not only for migrant workers, but also for other low-income urban groups, such as college students, white-collar workers in low-paid jobs, taxi drivers, and small business owners.

The majority of migrants list convenience as the top reason for choosing to live in ViCs (Zhang, 2005). ViCs contain a variety of retail and service establishments to meet the everyday demands of migrant workers, such as cheap grocery stores, noodle shops, barber shops, and telephone booths for making long-distance calls. Most buildings have at least basic amenities such as tap water, heating, electricity, gas, private kitchens, and toilets, and therefore migrants find ViCs much more attractive as a place to settle compared to remote rural areas without such modern utilities.

Shenzhen: a city of ViCs

Shenzhen is one of the cities in the Pearl River Delta with a large number of ViCs. In 1985, *hukou* restrictions were relaxed to allow rural migrant workers to register as temporary residents in urban areas, and this facilitated large-scale migration to Shenzhen. The population of Shenzhen in 1979 was only about 30,000; by 2010, the resident population had reached 10.36 million, among which 2.52 million had Shenzhen *hukou*.[4] A large number of migrants have settled in hundreds of ViCs in the city. According to Wang et al. (2009), there were 241 ViCs in Shenzhen in 2005, and, in Futian district alone, there were 15 ViCs occupying 390 hectares of land and housing 572,100 migrants.

The Shenzhen government's stance toward ViCs has changed over time, from the initial hands-off approach to the current model of redevelopment. According to Wang et al. (2009), in the first phase, between 1979 and 1992, the Shenzhen municipal government focused on developing new areas on the outskirts of the city where land was plentiful and the ownership was clear – that is, it was publicly owned. The city government did not want to demolish or redevelop the villages that stood in the way of the city's outward expansion; due to its limited financial capacity at the time, it did not want to bear the burden of taking care of villagers' social welfare needs in order to acquire their land. As the city expanded outward, some villages were quickly surrounded by urban development and became "islands" in the city. Because of their convenient location – i.e., they are now within city limits and some ViCs are even next to the Central Business District, villagers saw economic opportunity in developing and renting out properties to migrant workers, and quickly shifted from farming to property development on the collectively owned cropland.

In the second phase, between 1992 and 2002, the Shenzhen municipal government began to systematically "urbanize" ViCs within the city limits. In 1992 alone, 68 administrative village committees and 173 natural village committees were transformed into urban Resident Committees, and the *hukou* status of villagers was changed from agricultural to non-agricultural. Once the government acquires village land and compensates for the land loss of villagers with urban *hukou*, it often collaborates with real-estate companies to redevelop entire ViCs by building high-rise and market-rate commercial properties. As most existing structures are demolished in the redevelopment, painstaking negotiations are often carried out between developers, governments, and villager-landlords to determine which buildings are "legal" and how much the compensation should be (Wang et al., 2009).

In the current phase, since 2003, the city government has begun a campaign to urbanize all ViCs, especially those in the outlying Longgang and Bao'an districts (Wang et al., 2009). This has met strong resistance from ViCs, as many villagers are reluctant to let go of their rural *hukou*. Many ViCs in Shenzhen are still home to many migrants, but, in most cases, the transition of land ownership has been completed. By 2004, Shenzhen had become the first city in China to eliminate rural administration and the official agricultural population. At least in name, Shenzhen is completely urbanized. Now as the land is mostly state-owned, villagers have lost their collective ownership to land, but their ownership over self-built housing is legally recognized – they have 70 years of ownership rights over their built properties. The changing land ownership – from collectively owned to state-owned – makes ViCs vulnerable targets for redevelopment, as it is easier for the city government to relocate residents and demolish existing buildings on state land.

Density

The built form of ViCs in Shenzhen reflects villagers' resistance to the government's efforts to restrain ViC developments. Wang et al. (2009) note that since the 1980s, each and every effort by the city government – whether it is to restrict building activities or to legalize some of the illegally built structures – has triggered a building boom. Government restrictions have often led to panics and consequent building rushes, and legalization measures have encouraged villagers to build more. As a result, most ViCs have become densely built migrant enclaves with narrow alleys between tall buildings. The buildings are built so close to one another that residents joke that people in nearby buildings can kiss and shake hands with each other. In the 1980s, the government issued construction quotas per person, but villagers simply ignored the quotas. In the mid-1990s, the city government suspended approvals for new building construction permits, but the suspension was ignored again, and villagers went ahead to build more without permits. In 2001, the city government legalized unauthorized buildings and imposed fines on farmer landlords who had built too high or too much. But the fines were negligible compared to the profits from rental income, and the legalization only encouraged villagers to build even more. Once a ViC is slated for redevelopment – carried out by private developers and often with the local government providing infrastructure and amenities – it is often replaced by an extremely high-density residential and commercial complex because the developers need to pay relocation and compensation fees to villager-landlords, and to cover these costs and make a profit, they have no choice but to build denser and higher still.

Urban renewal coming to Shenzhen

Compared to other large cities such as Beijing and Shanghai, Shenzhen might be exceptional in its hands-off treatment of ViCs. Beijing and Shanghai initiated massive campaigns and demolished hundreds of ViCs in each city. Shenzhen, however, still retains a large number of ViCs in spite of the government's effort to incorporate them. Geographer You-Tien Hsing (2010) noted the exceptional strength of village associations in cities in southern China. Many ViCs, including in Shenzhen, have managed to maintain relative autonomy by setting up shareholding companies to collectively manage rental properties. Wang et al. (2009) argue that it is both the resistance from villagers and the reluctance of the city government to bear the burden of redevelopment costs, relocation, and the social welfare needs of villagers that have kept ViCs in place.

As the available cropland has been exhausted, developers and the city government have been increasingly eyeing the residential land on which villagers have built rental properties, and the pressure to redevelop ViCs has been mounting higher and higher. Beginning in 2004, the Shenzhen city government has passed a number of comprehensive plans aimed at redeveloping ViCs.[5] As happened in Beijing and Shanghai in the 1990s, Shenzhen, a city with only 30 years of history, has already begun to "renew" its "old" city quarters, such as ViCs, turning them into higher-value-added commercial and residential developments. In 2010, the city party secretary Wang Rong announced a list of 60 large-scale redevelopment projects, and 20 of them involved ViCs.[6]

From villagers to billionaires

Gangsha village is the last ViC to be redeveloped in the Central Business District of Shenzhen. The plan to redevelop the area had already been made by the city government as early as 1998, but it was halted for over 10 years because of compensation-related disputes. In 2002, the city government ordered the Futian district government to take charge of redevelopment, and four years later, in 2006, the city government signed a contract with a private developer to co-invest and develop the area. As demolition was about to begin in 2007, a local family named Cai did not agree with the compensation terms and took the government and the developer to court. The court, siding with the government and the developer, issued an eviction notice but the family refused to leave. The situation changed favorably for the Cai family when the central government passed the landmark Property Rights Law in 2007, and the Ministry of Land ordered local authorities not to use force to evict residents. After another round of negotiations, the developer finally agreed to offer 12 million RMB (about 1.9 million USD) to compensate the property loss of the Cai family. This astronomical compensation figure sent a shock wave through other villagers facing relocation. In Gangsha village, the percentage of villagers who had agreed to compensation terms suddenly dropped from 85 to 50 percent, and more people began to renegotiate with the developer for better terms. When demolition and construction finally began in 2009, after all residents agreed to take compensation and leave, the redevelopment project had already created 10 billionaires and 400 millionaires in the village (Chen, 2011).

Migrant housing needs

As seen in the story of Gangsha village in Shenzhen, the government stance toward ViCs has changed over time. Currently, redevelopment – compensating villagers at the market rate, demolishing existing structures, and building high-volume commercial projects – has become the predominant model of urbanizing ViCs. Although they are a minority, some villager-landlords have made a fortune from compensation fees, due to their strengthened negotiating power, combined with the order of the central government forbidding forced demolitions. However, the housing conditions of migrant tenants have only worsened as ViCs are redeveloped.

The relatively humane "redevelopment" approach – as compared to forced demolition and eviction without fair compensation – does not take into account the housing needs of migrant tenants living in ViCs. Migrant tenants are evicted when a ViC is redeveloped, and as there are few other housing options in the city, ViC redevelopment has sharply reduced the stock of affordable rental housing in the city and led to sharp increases in rents. Unable to find affordable accommodations in the city, some migrants have to relocate to places far away from the center, or give up their urban dream and go back to the countryside. In recent years, in large cities such as Beijing and Shanghai, urban residents often find "surprise" guests living in the parking garages, basements, and storage rooms of their apartment buildings.[7] The migrant housing situation has become desperate as the government continues to "redevelop" existing ViCs and ignore migrant housing needs.

LABOR CONDITIONS AND PROTESTS

Migrant workers come to cities to chase their dreams but, once there, they often find themselves stuck in low-paid and dead-end jobs without much hope of climbing the socio-economic ladder. Only a very small proportion of migrants work in professional jobs; the majority work in labor-intensive sectors such as construction, assembly-line manufacturing, and urban service industries, as taxi drivers, janitors, nannies, security guards, street vendors, and waiters and waitresses. In the manufacturing sector, most migrants work in foreign-invested and private enterprises, instead of state-owned enterprises with better benefits. Geographer Cindy Fan (2008) notes that even when migrants do get jobs in state factories, they are often hired as short-term contract workers without any access to benefits. During the 2008 recession, migrant workers were hit the hardest. There were more than 67,000 factory closures, and many factories were closed without any warning and without paying workers' wages.[8] In early 2009, more than 23 million migrant workers were unemployed, which was about 16.4 percent of the total migrant labor force at the time. The government encouraged migrants to go back to the countryside, but many of them are second-generation migrants who were born in the 1980s and 1990s. They grew up in cities and see themselves as urbanites, but do not have social welfare benefits as enjoyed by urban residents. With little experience in farming or exposure to the rural life, the second-generation migrants would face tremendous difficulties in adjusting to life back in the countryside. Different from their parents' generation, the younger generation is also more technology-savvy, rebellious, and less willing to "eat bitterness" (*chiku*) – a Chinese expression meaning enduring hardships. Most labor protests today involve second-generation migrants, and the mobilization is heavily dependent on cell-phone use, texting, and social media such as *weibo* – the Chinese equivalent of Twitter.

Labor rights abuse

Compared to non-migrants or permanent migrants (i.e., those who have acquired a local *hukou*), temporary migrants have the lowest income, even with education and occupation factors controlled for. Fan (2008) argues that this is a result of a deliberate effort on the part of the state to channel migrant workers to low-paid and informal job sectors. Discriminatory hiring, based on age, gender, and ethnicity, is also commonplace in the migrant labor market. For many assembly-line jobs, such as sewing clothes, toys, or shoes, or assembling computer parts and iPhones, many employers only hire unmarried young women below a certain age because they are believed to be more obedient and to be in better health to endure the taxing work. Many workers live in employer-provided dorms behind barbed-wire factory gates, a spatial arrangement that makes it easier for employers to impose long working hours and also keep migrants isolated from the urban life outside.

The *hukou* status of migrant workers makes them easy targets for exploitation, and labor rights abuses are widespread in the migrant labor market – for example, no pay, below-minimum wages, delayed wages, work injuries due to lack of safety training, and long working hours. The State Council conducted a survey of migrant labor conditions in 2006, which found that only 12.5 percent had signed a contract, only 10 percent had medical coverage, less than 48 percent were paid regularly, and 68 percent had never been paid overtime wages (Friedman and Lee, 2010). To improve the desperate working conditions of migrant workers and better protect their rights, the State Council passed a significant number of laws, beginning with the National Labor Law in 1995, which requires employers in all types of enterprises to sign a formal labor contract with their employees. This is reinforced in the Labor Contract Law of 2007, which imposes the universal requirement of a labor contract. The Employment Promotion Law of 2007 aims to reduce discriminatory hiring practices based on age, gender, and ethnicity, and the Labor Dispute Mediation and Arbitration Law in the same year set up guidelines for resolving labor disputes and streamlining arbitration processes. These State Council documents have specified minimum wage levels, workplace-injury compensation procedures, and medical coverage and pension rules; however, as Friedmann and Lee (2010) argue, these higher-level policies do not get implemented because local governments have their own regulations regarding social welfare benefits, and they often exclude migrant workers based on their *hukou* status.

The mega-factory: Foxconn

In 2010, Foxconn, a Taiwanese-owned electronics manufacturer, appeared in the news headlines worldwide, as 18 of its employees in different factory facilities across China jumped from dormitory buildings to commit suicide, one after another. Since it set up its first factory in Shenzhen in 1988, Foxconn has quickly grown into the world's largest electronics manufacturer. Foxconn is a paradigmatic example of China's factory-labor regime, typified by the consolidation of mega-factories, fierce competition among local governments to lure such enterprises, and harsh working and living conditions imposed on their workers. Following the Foxconn suicides, sociologists Pun Ngai and Jenny Chan conducted surveys and interviews with the workers, and studied production and reproduction at the world's largest electronics maker (Ngai and Chan, 2012).

Ngai and Chan noted that foreign-invested enterprises in light manufacturing used to be small and medium-sized, but mega-factories with multiple production sites in different cities have recently emerged in China, through mergers and expansion, and by taking advantage of local governments' generous offers of tax abatement, land, and labor supply in their bids for such investment. Foxconn set up its first workshop in Shenzhen in 1988, employing about 150 workers mostly from the same province, Guangdong. In the 1990s, the company rapidly expanded production and consolidated in the urban regions in the Pearl River Delta and Yangtze River Delta. Lured by the cheaper cost of labor and land, as well as by local government incentives, the company has opened more factories in western and central provinces since 2000. By aggressively competing with rival companies and by relocating to the western provinces, Foxconn has quickly become the largest electronics maker in the world, with production facilities in 11 cities across the country – Shenzhen, Wuhan, Kunshan, Shanghai, Hangzhou, Nanjing, Tianjin, Langfang, Taiyuan, Chengdu, and Chongqing. Its sales revenues reached 101 billion USD in 2010, higher than those of many of its multinational corporate clients, such as Dell and Nokia. Foxconn makes a great variety of electronics, from iPhones and iPads to desktop and laptop computers, digital cameras, TV sets and DVD players.

What sets Foxconn apart from other light electronics manufactures is the enormous size of its workforce – the company employs 1 million workers as of 2012. Mega-factories of such scale are unprecedented in history, even in China, and they are products of a combination of factors, including globalized manufacturing, cheap labor costs, and local government incentives. Even the smallest Foxconn factories employ 20,000 workers, and the largest one – Shenzhen Longhua – has a workforce of more than 430,000 people. In Shenzhen, Foxconn owns 33 company dorms and rents another 120 dorms in nearby communities to house its workers. Ngai and Chan report that the Longhua factory campus has a number of additional amenities that other Foxconn factories do not have, such as swimming pools, a basketball court, a theater, a library, and track and field facilities, and the company uses it as a showcase for government delegations, inspectors, and the media.

Life inside the world's largest electronics maker is harsh, especially for its young assembly-line workers. According to Ngai and Chan's questionnaire survey, the average age of the workers is only 21, indicating that most workers are second-generation migrants. Ten-hour workdays are normal, and the basic monthly wage in 2010 was between 147 and 186 USD. In addition to dealing with long hours, mind-bogglingly repetitive work, and mistreatment by management on the shop floor, the frontline workers are also pressured to meet tight deadlines when rush orders come in from multinational clients. For example, Ngai and Chan write that when Apple tried to get the new white model of its iPhone4 out to the market while keeping up the supply of the black model, workers had to pull 24-hour shifts to meet the demand. As of 2010, Longhua factory alone could make as many as 137,000 iPhones in a 24-hour workday. The work intensity and pressure leave little time for workers to rest and socialize after work, and many workers report high levels of alienation, exhaustion, and desperation. The 2010 suicides of the 18 workers, aged between 17 and 25, shocked the country and made Foxconn a household name overnight. To prevent more suicides, the company installed a total of 3 million square meters of netting to cover the outdoor stairways of all the dorms.

Rights-based mobilization

In contrast to such desperate measures as suicide, the labor rights abuses have also led to other and more active forms of resistance, such as litigations through the court, strikes on the shop floor, and open protests on the streets. In earlier phases until the mid-2000s, most labor protests had asked employers to pay delayed wages and unpaid wages, instead of demanding higher wages. Labor scholar and activist Anita Chan described this phenomenon as "rights-based" rather than "interest-based" resistance, which means that workers stage protests or seek legal means to assert their rights as already guaranteed by law, rather than making new demands (Chan, 2011). But interest-based protests demanding higher wages and better treatment have begun to appear recently. In 2010, workers in a Honda factory in Beijing went on strike to demand a 60 percent increase in wages, and after rounds of negotiations, the employer agreed to give workers a 24 percent raise. This seems like a great victory for workers, but Chan (2011) notes that the Beijing city government had ordered a 20 percent increase in the minimum wage before the negotiations took place, so the Honda factory actually offered workers only a 4 percent raise. Nevertheless, the much publicized Honda factory strike is the first "interest-based" labor strike in China's factories.

Rights-based claims-making is a central feature of urban social movements throughout China, and migrant workers have increasingly used the law as their weapon, asserting their labor rights as guaranteed by state laws, policies, and regulations. Political scientists Kevin O'Brien and Lianjiang Li (2006) coined the term "rightful resistance" to describe the rhetoric of rights in protesters' framing of their cause. The rights-based claims-making has to do with the promulgation of a large number of labor laws around 2007, described in the previous section. But it also has to be explained in relation to the transition from work-unit-based social contracts to market-based labor contracts, as argued by labor sociologist C. K. Lee. Lee (2007) compares labor protests by two groups of workers – laid-off and retired workers in northeastern Liaoning province, and young migrant workers in Guangdong. She finds that the older generation of laid-off workers tends to take to the streets to vent their grievances, while the younger generation of migrant workers resort to legal activism against discrimination. As she explains, the social contract in the socialist era was an implicit exchange between the state and workers, the terms of which were not specified in any legal document. Most workers in state-owned work units were lifetime employees, and in return for their labor and loyalty to the party and the workplace, they received the whole basket of social welfare benefits. In the reform era, however, the implicit social contract of lifetime employment is replaced by a market-based labor contract, which is backed by a large number of legal documents and government regulations. Therefore, when disputes arise, workers tend to resort to the law to claim their legally guaranteed rights, in addition to organizing protests and strikes.

The practice of rights-based claims-making has developed in the larger context of the government promotion of the rule of law and the transition from the socialist to the market-based labor contract. But, as workers in China are not allowed to organize their own unions, and the official unions are de facto government agencies and do not really represent workers' interests, over time rights-based claims-making has increasingly taken on an extremely individualized character. Workers are encouraged by the government to seek legal means or use the bureaucratic system of arbitration to fight for their *individual* rights – to better working conditions, wages, or injury compensation – instead of *collective* rights. This individualization of collective problems significantly constrains the potential of labor movements in China, as it basically directs powerless individual migrant workers to enter the bureaucratic maze of arbitration and litigation, and to confront the extremely powerful state.

When legal means fail, the last resort for workers is to walk out of the factories, go to the streets, and engage in direct confrontation with employers and local authorities. In the past, most of such open confrontations were met with strong repression by the state. Chan (2011) compares workers' protests in Taiwanese-owned footwear factories in China and in Vietnam. She finds that Taiwanese investors do not see labor protests in China as a problem, because they know that in China the local governments will always side with investors, while in Vietnam they do take labor complaints seriously, because the government is on the side of workers and the trade unions are relatively strong. Taiwanese bosses treat workers in Vietnam better than those in China as a result of the different attitude of each government. Chan (2011) concludes that in China workers are subject to "soft laws, harsh punishments," while in Vietnam it is "harsh laws, soft implementations." Although law in China does not acknowledge the rights to association and to organized strikes, neither is illegal. The government has deliberately left this area a gray zone. But when strikes occur, even though they are not technically illegal, the authorities nevertheless suppress them harshly, with leaders often put in jail. In Vietnam, there are strong regulations discouraging workers from organizing protests and strikes, but when strikes do happen – and they happen quite often – the government often sides with workers and does not issue harsh punishments.

As the central government is concerned with social stability more than ever, and as labor protests become better organized and more confrontational, the state response to labor protests has shown a number of signs of change, such as a move from repression to containment and accommodation. In 2008, a senior official of the central government, Zhou Yongkang, announced two principles instructing how local governments should handle protests. The first is preemption – local officials should do what they can to prevent protests from happening in the first place. The second is immediate action – local government agencies such as the police, the court, and labor bureaus should be on the site of protests immediately after they break out. In addition, Zhou also warned about using violence to crack down on protesters (Su and He, 2010). In response to the order from the central government, there has been some noticeable change on the part of local governments in their handling of labor protests. For example, Su and He (2010) observed that local courts and government agencies have been increasingly engaging protesters in the streets and trying to find solutions favorable to protesters. In the case when foreign factory owners fled the country without paying workers' wages, local courts had to somehow find money to compensate workers by themselves, from all kinds of sources, such as village collectives that lease land to factories and neighborhood committees. Also, most local governments in the Pearl River Delta have a special reserve of emergency funds, called "stability maintenance budgets," with which they pay angry protesters and disperse crowds. As described by Su and He (2010), "the street has become the courtroom" and court staffs behave like "firefighters or combat soldiers," as a result of the pressure from the central government to maintain stability and the weak capacity of legal institutions.

The massive labor-rights abuses have produced vast discontent and led to a large number of strikes and protests across the country. In spite of the weak capacity of China's legal institutions, the state has been actively advocating "the rule of law" by encouraging workers to seek legal means to fight for their rights. This unique configuration of labor, legal, and political conditions has turned labor movements in China into individualized claims-making, as workers struggle through the bureaucratic maze of petition (*xinfang*), arbitration, and litigation to defend their rights. The individualization of collective rights has led to a proliferation of legal aid clinics and labor NGOs. As we shall see in the next section, these organizations have greatly facilitated workers in their fight for better protection of labor rights, but at the same time, operating within the space designed by the state, they also perpetuate the individualistic character of the migrant workers' rights movement.

MIGRANT NGOS

The state is unwilling and unable to attend to the welfare needs of migrant workers, and the workers' *hukou* status has made them vulnerable targets for exploitation. Since the early 2000s, an increasing number of non-government organizations (NGOs) have appeared in China to address the labor and welfare issues faced by migrant workers. In 2002–3, the central government called for the protection of the legal rights of migrant workers, and this change in the state stance toward migrants has since opened up opportunities for migrant NGOs.

Most migrant NGOs work in three areas – providing legal aid for migrant workers in labor disputes; delivering services such as education for migrants' children, vocational training, and medical help; and building solidarity and facilitating social networking among migrant workers by organizing cultural events. Many migrant NGOs receive funding from overseas foundations, individual foreign donors, and foreign embassies in China, and over the past few years they have quickly become the leading advocacy groups working on behalf of migrants to improve their labor conditions in the city.

There are three major types of migrant NGOs in terms of organizational origins (Froissart, 2006; Hsu, 2007). The first type is known as GONGOs (Government Organized NGOs), referring to those sponsored by the government and working as extensions of the state, such as Beijing Dagongmei Zhijia – an NGO working for migrant women's rights and affiliated with the All China Women's Federation. Second, there are migrant NGOs founded by urban residents and not directly affiliated with any state organization. Examples of this type include Facilitator, a migrant NGO based in Beijing and Nanjing, and Friends of Migrant Workers, a legal clinic based at Sun Yat-Sen University in Guangzhou. Third, migrant workers have also founded their own NGOs – for example, Xiaoxiaoniao Hotline (Beijing, Shenyang and Shenzhen), Zaixingdong (Beijing and Suzhou),

Gongyou Zhijia (Beijing), and the Institute of Contemporary Observation (Shenzhen). Due to the onerous requirements set up by the state for NGO registration, such as endorsement from a state organization, most NGOs are registered as enterprises with the Bureau of Industry and Commerce, instead of as NGOs with the Ministry of Civil Affairs.

By far the largest numbers of migrant NGOs are concentrated in Beijing and Shenzhen. The NGOs in Beijing are diverse and have extensive international connections. Their activities go beyond providing legal aid to delivering services and organizing cultural activities to facilitate socialization among migrants and to help them better integrate into urban life. Ironically but unsurprisingly, the most progressive labor NGOs – those trying to organize workers and eventually change the system – are found in Shenzhen, the first Special Economic Zone in the country. The Shenzhen-based NGOs mostly focus on labor disputes, for example, offering legal aid to migrant workers and helping them with labor arbitration. Many of the labor NGOs in Shenzhen have close ties with activist groups across the border in Hong Kong and with international organizations. The Institute of Contemporary Observation (ICO) is one of the oldest labor NGOs in Shenzhen, founded in 2001. According to statistics compiled by ICO, from 2001 to 2005, the organization carried out training programs for worker–employer relationship management in 15 factories, set up internal complaint mechanisms in more than 500 factories, conducted corporate social responsibility audits in 150 factories, provided legal aid to over 10,000 migrant workers, and offered vocational training to 1,500 workers. The number of workers who have benefited from ICO's various programs exceeds 200,000.[9]

In spite of their contributions, the space of operations for migrant NGOs in China is largely constrained by the state, and this has to some extent undermined their ability to challenge the system. First, as political scientist Mary Gallagher (2004) points out, China's civic associations are tightly monitored by the state, through mechanisms such as legal and administrative guidelines, restricted financial autonomy, double posting of officials – government officials are often appointed as leaders in civic associations, and the ideological penetration of the party-state's ideology. All of these mechanisms apply in the case of migrant NGOs. For instance, the requirement of sponsorship by a state-sector work unit makes it difficult for many migrant NGOs without government connections to register. There have also been increasing restrictions on NGOs' ability to receive funding from overseas sources. For GONGOs, the double posting of officials is a widespread practice. The independent NGOs without government affiliations have to constantly court local governments in order to continue their activities. Over time, some of these NGOs have become transmission belts of the party-state, as described by Froissart (2006), helping to foster the official ideology and exert social control over migrant workers.

The second major limitation of migrant NGOs is their strong orientation toward service delivery. The services delivered by migrant NGOs, such as legal aid, medical care, and children's education, have unquestionably improved the working and living conditions of migrant workers in the city. Local governments encourage and support such NGO activities, but crack down on NGOs when they engage in labor organizing, make political claims, or try to build coalitions among themselves. Beja (2006) argues that the NGOs in China in the 1990s and after did not play the same combative role as the ones that emerged in Eastern Europe and China in the 1980s. Many NGOs are humanitarian associations that seek to lobby the government to implement policies to solve specific problems. Beja (2006) notes that, instead of framing these problems – such as housing, migrant children's education, and labor rights abuses – in political terms so that they can be debated in public, NGOs tend to present them as technical problems and make policy recommendations for technical solutions.

The last major limitation of migrant NGOs is their perception, presentation, and solution of migrant workers' problems as individual problems instead of collective ones (Lee and Shen, 2009). As Friedman and Lee (2010) note, labor NGOs have been active participants in the state project of "rule of law," and by providing legal assistance and encouraging workers to sue their employers, the NGOs are individualizing the systemic problems of labor conflicts. This tendency has to do with the funding source of migrant NGOs – as many foreign donors and foundations are more likely to fund programs that promote the rule of law, rather than programs for labor mobilization and organizing, the NGOs tend to adopt a legalistic approach to labor-rights disputes.

In a case study on legal-aid services, Gallagher (2007) describes the paradoxes and dilemmas generated by this individualistic and legalistic approach of migrant NGOs. She notes that the legal aid services provided by labor NGOs help to heighten the legal consciousness of migrant workers, by making them more aware of their legally guaranteed rights. Overall, participation in legal-aid programs is an empowering experience for migrant workers. However, their chance of succeeding in court is fairly limited, because China's court system is already overburdened by the skyrocketing number of lawsuits and is not truly independent – many local courts work as de facto branches of the party-state.

Some of the limitations identified above are not unique to Chinese NGOs, and similar orientations can also be seen in urban social movements in the West, such as the shift in strategy from protest to program and service delivery, and claims-making for inclusion in the current system instead of challenging the status quo (Mayer, 2009). What makes the Chinese NGO sector unique is the very deliberate intervention of the state in shaping NGO activities – through both direct administrative restrictions and indirect measures – to encourage migrant NGOs to adopt an individualistic, legalistic, and service-oriented approach. It is tempting to jump to the conclusion that, due to these limitations, migrant NGOs are incapable of truly challenging the current labor regime and reformulating urban citizenship. However, it is overly simplistic to construct a dichotomy of state vs society, and frame the question in terms of whether civil society can overthrow the authoritarian Chinese state, or the state will trump civil society and maintain the status quo. Instead of viewing the state and civic associations as engaged in a zero-sum game, we need to examine how the state and civil society have mutually transformed one another. In the case of migrant NGOs, despite the severe constraints under which they operate, it is necessary to recognize their transformative potential. Briefly, I identify a number of such possibilities below.

First, the service delivery undertaken by migrant NGOs *is* challenging the current urban citizenship regime by expanding social rights to migrant workers, because citizenship in China is largely defined in terms of social rights – such as rights to education, training, work, housing, and welfare, as versus political and civil rights. The rural–urban inequality mostly concerns social rights – there is little difference in political and civil rights across the rural–urban divide, as these rights are fairly limited on both sides under the current one-party rule. Second, despite the limitations of NGOs' legalistic approach, the various legal-aid programs have greatly empowered migrant workers, heightened their rights awareness, and fostered a collective identity among them. In addition to the expanded services enjoyed by migrants, the heightened rights awareness provided by these programs is another major step toward reformulating urban citizenship and making the progression from social rights to political and civil rights. Furthermore, having these pockets of non-profit, democratic organizations in a non-democratic, non-electoral regime produces new sources of pressure and instability within the system, as argued by Gallagher (2007). For example, the legal-aid services provided by NGOs have generated a sense of "informed disenchantment" (Gallagher, 2007). Such bottom-up pressure, instability, and disenchantment have planted seeds for the future expansion of the right to the city.

CONCLUSIONS

This chapter has examined the trends in rural-to-urban migration in China, and the specific barriers migrants face in the urban housing and labor markets. In a seminal study on Chinese migrant workers in the 1980s and 1990s, Solinger (1999) correctly observes that citizenship does not come easily to migrants whose arrival coincided with marketization. A decade has passed since Solinger's study, and the situation has not changed much. The state and market mechanisms are still blocking migrants' claim to the citizenship rights enjoyed by their urban counterparts.

Although there are piecemeal reforms in the *hukou* system, *hukou* continues to serve the function of channeling cheap labor to the booming industrial regions while denying migrant workers urban citizenship rights. In the housing market, *hukou* prevents migrants from accessing many public-housing programs targeting low-income groups, and the skyrocketing housing prices put commodity housing out of their reach. Large numbers of migrants have settled in ViCs for their convenience and cheaper cost of living, but as local governments continue campaigns to urbanize and redevelop ViCs, the affordable housing options have become few and far between for migrants. The right to housing is a principal component of rights to urban life. The huge disparity in housing conditions between migrants and urbanites shows that migrants still have a long way to go to gain equal footing with their urban counterparts in their own country.

In the labor market, labor-rights violations have led to protests and strikes, and most such mobilizations make claims that are both rights-based (i.e., demanding rights guaranteed by existing laws) and interest-based (e.g., demanding better wages and working conditions). Due to the large number of labor laws passed in recent years, workers increasingly resort to the law as their weapon, asserting the rights that are guaranteed to them by law. However, the government promotion of the rule of law, together with the lack of civil rights to association, has fragmented the migrant workers' rights movement, turning it into a legalistic exercise of asserting individual, instead of collective, rights. In addition to seeking justice through legal channels, labor protests have become more violent and confrontational since 2010. As the pressure to maintain social stability mounts, local government officials have changed their strategies of handling protests, from repression by force to engaging protesters on the streets and trying to accommodate protesters' demands. Finally, the chapter has also examined the recent development of migrant NGOs. Although these NGOs still can only reach a small portion of migrants, they are helping migrants to challenge the current citizenship regime by filling the welfare gap, generating pressure within the system, and raising workers' rights consciousness. Although still underprivileged and marginalized, the millions of migrant workers in China are challenging the institutional urban–rural divide and asserting their right to the new Chinese city.

5 | Inequality ————————————————

China's market reform has created both extraordinary wealth and poverty, turning the country from a relatively egalitarian society into an extremely unequal one. The urban real-estate sector is one of the best places to observe how great fortunes are made for the few and unprecedented destitution descends upon the majority. Between 2005 and 2009, when I was doing fieldwork on the development of Beijing's new Central Business District, one real-estate developer – SOHO China – caught my attention. Different from many other developers with strong ties to the city government, SOHO China is a private firm founded by a husband-and-wife team in the late 1990s, and back then it did not have strong government connections. Pan Shiyi, the CEO of the company, graduated from a provincial college and worked as a government clerk in Gansu province – one of the poorest provinces in the country. He quit his state-sector job and went to Hainan – the epicenter of China's first real-estate bubble, in the 1990s. Together with a few other business partners, Pan made a small fortune by buying and selling real estate. After the bubble of Hainan's real-estate market burst spectacularly in 1993, leaving the island province dotted with unfinished buildings, Pan came to Beijing to seek new opportunities. In Beijing, he met his wife, Zhang Xin, who grew up in Mainland China, worked in a factory in Hong Kong, and later had the opportunity of studying at the University of Cambridge. After working for a short period on Wall Street, Zhang Xin came back to Beijing to seek new business opportunities. In the late 1990s, SOHO China acquired land from Beijing No.1 Machinery Factory – a bankrupt state-owned enterprise sitting right in the middle of the designated Central Business District. Factory workers were laid off, workshops were demolished, and, in just a few years, SOHO China turned the area into Jianwai SOHO, one of the most prestigious office addresses in Beijing, with a cluster of office and residential buildings designed by a Japanese architectural team. Operating on a design-intensive model – each and every one of its projects has been designed by renowned international architects – SOHO China has quickly developed into a real-estate empire, with a dozen development projects dotting the capital city and billions in annual sales revenues. Pan Shiyi and Zhang Xin are among the first generation of private entrepreneurs and billionaires in reform-era China.

SOHO China tells the story of how extreme wealth is produced in reform-era China and how the once-egalitarian society has become increasingly divided between the haves and have-nots. Alongside real-estate tycoons, urban development projects have also given birth to a new stratum of property owners who became extremely wealthy as real-estate prices in Beijing tripled and quadrupled in the single decade of the 2000s. Investors who had capital to buy SOHO properties in the Central Business District have made a fortune in a matter of just a few years, further deepening the gap between them and the vast urban poor – for example, the laid-off workers and the low-paid migrants laboring as construction workers, janitors, and security guards for the signature-designed, sleek buildings at Jianwai SOHO.

THE MARKET TRANSITION DEBATE

Social scientists have closely followed the rise of inequality in China, gathering statistics and developing theories to explain how resources are allocated differently under market reform than in the days of socialism. This scholarly inquiry into China's inequality led to a "market transition" debate in the 1990s between two competing explanations. On one side of the debate, scholars such as Victor Nee argued that the emergence of market institutions in socialist economies could reduce social inequality, as political connections are rewarded less than human capital and entrepreneurial skills. Nee's market-transition theory is based on a rural survey conducted in 1985, which found that between 1977 and 1985 rural income inequality declined substantially (Nee, 1989). On the other side of the debate, Andrew Walder and others argued that the historical and institutional legacies of the socialist era persisted in the transition period, and state organizations, rather than the market, would continue to be dominant in determining the life chances of individuals (Walder, 1992; Lin, 1995). According to this second perspective, individuals with close ties to the government and authorities still have better access to good housing, good jobs, and higher income than those without such political and social capital.

Both views in the market-transition debate are supported by data and evidence. To use the real-estate sector as a case, private developers such as Pan Shiyi and Zhang Xin have aggressively competed in the property market, and with their sharp business acumen and entrepreneurial skills, they have built a real-estate empire that changed the landscape of Beijing's Central Business District. Their ability and skills are handsomely rewarded in the market, as reflected in the revenues generated by the SOHO buildings. But private firms without strong government connections, such as SOHO China in its founding years, are the minority, and most major players in the real-estate sector are still either state-owned companies or private companies headed by CEOs who have close ties to the government or who are themselves former government officials. The market-transition debate offered two polarized views that attribute the causes of differential allocations of resources to *either* market *or* state factors. But, in reality, the empirical evidence often supports both views; that is, in transitional China, both market capabilities and government connections – and the interactions between the two – can enable certain groups of people to get rich much faster than the rest and produce social inequality.

As the market reform has entered its fourth decade, and major institutional reforms have significantly restructured individuals' access to capital and resources, the simplified dichotomy of state vs market is no longer useful to explain the causes, patterns, and trajectories of social inequality. By the end of the 2000s, multiple historical and institutional factors had produced a very complex picture of social stratification. As sociologists Deborah Davis and Feng Wang (2009) suggest, there is no overarching theory that can explain the complex picture of the new social inequality in China today. Both historical legacies and institutional context matter, and "it is social and political context, and the interaction of individual attributes within organizational settings that define the current patterns of stratification" (2009: 5).

MAJOR TRENDS IN INEQUALITY

Three major trends in inequality can be identified in the constantly changing landscape of social stratification in China today. First, absolute poverty has declined but the gap between the rich and poor has widened. No matter what measures are used – income, consumption, or caloric intake – there has been a significant drop in absolute poverty over the period of the market reform, and half of the decline occurred in the first few years of the reform, in the 1980s (Davis and Wang, 2009). Absolute poverty rates continued to drop throughout the 1990s. For example, using a poverty line of 2 USD per day, poverty in the overall national population of China dropped from 7.3 percent in 1995 to 2.1 percent in 2002 (Appleton and Song, 2007). Meanwhile, the gap between the rich and poor has widened rapidly. In the early 1980s, China's Gini Index was less than 0.3 – with zero being total equality and one being total inequality. This was much lower than the scores of most developed and developing countries at that time, but, by the 1990s, the Gini Index had increased to 0.39, bypassing many countries (Wang, 2008).

Second, a large and increasing new urban underclass of the unemployed, the laid-off, and low-paid workers has emerged. Examining the period of the early 2000s, Dorothy Solinger noted that around 20 to 30 million registered urban residents (i.e., with urban *hukou*) had fallen into poverty; accounting for their families, the total number would be around 40 to 50 million. This did not take into account migrant workers, who numbered between 150 and 200 million. About 15 to 20 percent of migrant workers in cities lived below the poverty line. So, added all together, Solinger estimated that as many as 70 million Chinese lived in poverty in the first half of the 2000s (Solinger, 2006).

Third, there has been an increasing divide between property-owning and propertyless classes, and properties such as housing are further fragmenting urban Chinese society. By 2010, the rate of homeownership among registered urban residents had already reached 72.5 percent.[1] Although specific statistics are not available, it is certain that the new urban poor have a very low rate of homeownership – for example, homeownership among migrant workers is still below 1 percent today. As real-estate prices keep rising in cities across the country, the divide between the two classes is widening too. The increasing inequality in housing will have significant implications for future generations (Wang, 2008).

In addition to economic restructuring and changes in social welfare, urban renewal and redevelopment has also been a major mechanism producing new wealth and poverty, and this mechanism is often neglected in social stratification studies (Chen, Gu and Wu, 2006). This chapter examines how all three of these factors have produced new patterns of inequality in reform-era China, especially since 2000. The first section will map major patterns of *social* inequality, based on work done by sociologists who have studied how individual attributes such as gender, education, and political status determine access to better jobs, better housing, and higher income. The second section will shift to an examination of *spatial* inequality, introducing major work done in recent years by geographers who have studied the spatial distribution of inequality at the community and neighborhood levels. Lastly, based on my own fieldwork in Beijing and Shanghai in the second half of the 2000s, I will closely examine how urban renewal programs have generated spectacular wealth for the fortunate few and displaced the vast majority from the urban center, exacerbating the systemic social stratification in today's China.

SOCIAL INEQUALITY

Most sociological studies on stratification in China have focused on identifying the types of *individual* attributes such as gender, age groups, and education that are better rewarded. Only recently, sociologists have begun to pay attention to *categorical* attributes, such as living in a particular city or being employed in a particular economic sector, in shaping individual life chances, thus offering new insights on social inequality in the country. This section examines both the individual approach and the categorical approach to studying social inequality.

Gender

China has a long history of extreme gender inequality, with women being blocked from education, free marriage, and employment outside the household. One of the biggest achievements of socialism was to reverse the previous unequal gender relations and make women into new socialist citizens just like their male counterparts. Under socialism, women were found working in all economic sectors and occupations, and the wage differential between men and women was small compared to other countries. But recent studies show that gender inequality and discrimination have been resurfacing during the market reform. Based on a survey on income inequality in the period between 1986 and 2000, Cohen and Wang (2008) find that the gender gap in income increased rapidly in that period and women were more likely to work in low-paid jobs. Female urban workers earned about 15 percent less than male workers in the early 1980s but, by the end of the 2000s, the gap had widened to 25 percent. The gender gap is also found to be larger in more developed cities, probably due to the wider range of economic sectors and occupations and their associated pay levels, and the state sector offers better protection for women than the private sector.

In addition to the widening income gap, gender inequality is also reflected in the lower numbers of women occupying high-level positions in both private enterprises and government organizations. Guthrie (2008) cites a survey conducted by the Chinese Academy of Social Sciences and reports that men account for about three-quarters of the dominant positions, such as state officials and managers in state and private enterprises. The higher up the organizational hierarchy, the fewer women can be found. In the public sector, women have to retire at age 55, and this prevents many experienced female officials and professionals from obtaining high-rank positions. On the other end of the occupational hierarchy, women typically make up 70 to 80 percent of the laid-off and unemployed. Facing tremendous difficulty in getting rehired, a large number of laid-off women either remain unemployed or find low-paid work in the informal sector.

Education

The higher-education system in China has rapidly expanded since 1995, when then-president Jiang Zemin called for the development of science, technology, and education. This renewed emphasis is reflected in government spending on education and research. According to Wang et al. (2011), from 1997 to 2007, government spending on education increased from 33.4 billion RMB to 164.8 billion RMB, at an annual growth rate of 13 percent; college enrollment increased from 3 million students in 1997 to 17 million in 2007; and, while only 3.4 percent of high-school seniors went to college in 1997, the number jumped to 22 percent 10 years later, which means that now more than one out of five students of high-school age pursues higher education. The national education reform in the late 1990s focused on building "One Hundred Key Universities" that would receive targeted state funding in order to be able to compete internationally. To get into the top 100, smaller colleges merged with larger research universities in the late 1990s. As a result, the number of higher-education institutions declined slightly at the time, but the size of major Chinese universities became much larger than before, with multiple campuses and more students enrolled. Among the top 100, 10 universities were selected in 1998 as "international-level" universities and given targeted funding from the central government, and the rest are supported by provincial and municipal governments (Guthrie, 2008). The elite universities at the very top, such as Peking, Tsinghua, and Fudan, can also receive extra funding and are encouraged to reach out to, collaborate, and compete with other top schools in the world. Overall, China has developed a highly stratified structure of higher education, with elite schools receiving the lion's share of government research funding.

The expansion of the university system has offered more opportunities for the country's younger generation to receive higher education; however, the opportunities are not evenly distributed across social groups, as defined by gender, ethnicity, socio-economic status, and *hukou*. A group of researchers associated with REAP (the Rural Education Action Project) at Stanford University conducted a survey of over 20,000 freshmen at four universities in 2008 in three provinces – Anhui, Sichuan, and Shanxi. The schools surveyed included two nationally supported universities (Xi'an Jiaotong University and Sichuan University) and two provincial colleges (Anhui University and Northwest University in Xi'an). The researchers described the Chinese college as "a rich, Han, urban, and male club" (Wang et. al., 2011). They find that there is still systematic under-representation of women, ethnic minorities, and the rural poor in the country's four-year colleges. The sharpest inequality in access to higher education is found between well-off urban students in large cities and poor rural students. In 2006, 54 percent of high-school students in Beijing, Shanghai, and Tianjin went to a four-year college – 32 percent higher than the national average – but only 4 percent of students from poor families in rural areas were able to do the same. The urban–rural bias is more evident in elite, nationally supported colleges than at provincial colleges. Moreover, rural women are the most under-represented group in Chinese colleges. In rural areas, girls are often discouraged from going to high school even in well-off families, and, in less well-off families, parents often pool resources to support their sons' education and send their daughters to work at a young age.

Based on another survey of 1,177 high-school students from eight poor counties in Shanxi province, the same research team studied why the rural poor have been systematically excluded from China's higher-education system. They found that the barriers to college education for the rural poor lie not in the phase of high schools or college admission exams, but can be traced to the low quality of preschools and elementary schools in rural areas, poor nutrition, the low quality of boarding facilities, the high costs of high school, and the instability of migrant schools outside the public education system (Wang et al., 2011).

Political status

In addition to gender and education, researchers in the field of stratification in China have also closely examined to what extent political status – such as party membership, or position and rank in government organizations or state-owned enterprises – is still rewarded in the market transition. Previous studies in the early 1990s showed consistent evidence of a significant role for political status (Bian and Logan, 1996), but, as time passes, the picture has become less clear. Some have studied the impact of political status on housing inequality – housing can be a better measure than income in studying the effects of political status, since government officials in China have fixed salaries but receive a large number of perks and benefits such as housing. Logan, Bian, and Bian (1999) examined the effects of political status (measured by positions of authority held and connections with officials), work unit affiliations, and socio-economic variables on housing conditions (measured by square meters per capita and amenities). They found that all three sets of variables were significant in determining individuals' housing conditions. Officials or those with close ties to officials, people working in better-resourced work units, and more senior, better-educated individuals tended to have larger housing space in better condition. The study is based on a survey conducted in 1993, when the main phase of the housing reform had not yet begun. In a later study, based on the 1995 One Percent Population Survey and the 2000 census, Huang and Jiang (2009) found different patterns from Logan, Bian, and Bian's earlier study. Their results showed that certain socialist institutions such as *hukou* are still significant factors contributing to housing inequality, but political status (e.g., the rank of heads of government agencies, party organizations, and state-owned enterprises) has lost much of its importance over the years in predicting housing conditions. In other words, different elements of the former socialist institutions have different impact in reproducing social inequality in the reform era – *hukou* is still a key factor in shaping individual life chances, but political status has begun to matter less.

Categorical inequality: employment and cities

While most sociological work on stratification focuses on the effects of *individual* attributes in determining life chances, recently a *categorical* approach to studying inequality has emerged. Based on a large-sample survey on income inequality in Shenyang, Guangzhou, and Chongqing in 2000, Wang (2008) finds that there has been increasing inequality *between* groups and relative egalitarianism *within* groups. "Groups" are defined by, for example, employment status – the urban unemployed, migrant workers, professionals, etc.; place of residence – people living in the same city; type of employer – workers in private enterprises or state enterprises; and industrial sector – manufacturing workers, service workers, etc. Wang (2008) notes that a large portion of inequality is found *between* these groups instead of *within* them. He argues that this is due to the differential positions of social categories, which in turn derive from China's cultural and institutional tendency to privilege group membership and within-group egalitarianism. An example of within-group equality can be found in the case of the urban working class under socialism. Although there was a great deal of variation in individual attributes, urban workers under socialism had more or less the same standards of living and access to welfare resources. As the reform of SOEs deepened in the 1990s, a large number of urban workers were laid off, and they have had great difficulty in finding new jobs, regardless of their expertise and experience. Thus, by virtue of being a member of the category of the former urban working class, one is subject to a significantly higher likelihood of experiencing lay-off and unemployment than members of other categories, simply because the category of state-sector urban workers drifted to a disadvantaged position during the economic restructuring.

The city where one lives also has a significant impact on one's access to education and better-paid jobs. Wang's (2008) survey data show that "city" is a key variable in explaining income inequality among individuals, especially for the portion of income generated and regulated locally. Residents living in China's bigger cities also tend to have higher incomes than the rest of the population. Wang (2008) correctly argues that this is not because of different levels of development and costs of living, but because cities have emerged as highly independent political economic units with entrepreneurial government officials actively promoting local growth. The fiscal reform in the 1990s has decentralized decision-making authority to municipal governments, but also transferred many obligations and responsibilities to the local level, such as investment in infrastructure and provision of social welfare to urban residents. With enhanced power but also urgent pressure to cover expenses, municipal governments have liberally intervened in land development to expand their revenue sources (chapter 2). Together with taxes and fees arbitrarily levied on enterprises under their control, this development income makes up "extra-budgetary" revenues that do not have to be shared with the central government. These extra-budgetary revenues have gone in part to the income and welfare of local officials, and, to a lesser extent, to local residents as well (Wang, 2008). Driven by the rent-seeking behavior of local officials and power decentralized from the central government, Chinese cities are highly autonomous political economic units in a constant race to promote *local* growth, which has significant consequences on the life chances of urban residents.

SPATIAL INEQUALITY

While sociologists examine patterns of inequality from the perspective of individual and categorical attributes, urban geographers focus instead on the spatial distribution of inequality across neighborhoods. They first distinguish the old urban poor from the new urban poor, with the former including the "three-no" population in the socialist era – i.e., people with no income, no working capacity, and no family support, and the latter referring to the unemployed, the retired, and the working poor (Chen, Gu, and Wu, 2006). Compared to the limited size of the "three-no" population, the new urban poor are much greater in number, and they have begun to concentrate in particular types of neighborhoods. Specifically, geographers have identified three types of neighborhoods of poverty: the old inner-city neighborhoods, the degraded work-unit housing compounds, and migrant villages (Chen, Gu, and Wu, 2006; Liu and Wu, 2006; Wu, He, and Webster, 2010). About 20 to 30 percent of the resident population in these poverty neighborhoods live under the official poverty line defined by local governments, according to a six-city survey conducted in 2006 by geographer He Shenjing and colleagues – the cities included Xi'an, Guangzhou, Nanjing, Wuhan, Harbin, and Kunming (He et al., 2010).

Economic restructuring and changes in the social welfare regime are the leading causes of the emergence of the new urban poor. SOE reforms since the 1980s have produced a large number of unemployed workers, especially in cities that were industrial centers in the socialist era. Gone with the work units is the full package of social welfare services that they provided. Although economic restructuring has affected every city and neighborhood, urban poverty groups are not randomly distributed; rather, they tend to concentrate in specific neighborhoods. As the living conditions worsen, better-off families flee from these places to new commercial housing estates, and the neighborhoods left behind have gradually turned into pockets of deep poverty. The previous chapter has discussed migrant enclaves (i.e., ViCs), and this section will focus on the other two types of poverty neighborhoods – old inner-city neighborhoods and degraded workers' villages.

Old inner-city neighborhoods

In old inner-city neighborhoods, a mixture of housing-ownership schemes can be found. Some of the housing stock was built after 1949 and belongs to city governments, and others were built before 1949 and belong to private owners. When China abolished private owner-ship of housing, private housing stock was transferred to the hands of municipal housing authorities, and it only returned to private owner-ship after the 1980s. These neighborhoods were largely neglected and left to decay during the socialist years, as local governments had limited resources for neighborhood upgrading and most funding went to new construction of work-unit compounds in order to accommodate urban workers and their families. Due to the severe housing shortage between the 1950s and 1970s, many inner-city neighborhoods became densely populated, with multiple families often sharing one courtyard house that was designed for single-family use. Since the 1990s, a large number of these neighborhoods have been razed, and the residents dispersed. But to avoid high relocation and compensation costs, developers and local governments have bypassed some old inner-city neighborhoods with high population density and limited land. As the better-off fami-lies flee to newer neighborhoods, these old inner-city neighborhoods have quickly become poverty areas with a high percentage of the laid-off, the unemployed, and the working poor.

In a study on urban poverty in Nanjing, Liu and Wu (2006) described the transformation of *Pingshijie*, a typical old inner-city neighborhood, into a pocket of poverty over time. The neighborhood was built in the Ming dynasty in the fifteenth century and developed in the Qing dynasty. It was severely damaged during World War II and the Japanese invasion, as was the rest of Nanjing. Middle- to lower-income retailers and craftsmen gradually concentrated here in the Republican era, and when the Communist Party came to power, the residents were recruited as industrial workers in collectively owned enterprises in the neighborhood. In the socialist years, the industrial construction and investment bypassed *Pingshijie* and the rest of the old urban area altogether, and went instead to inner-ring suburbs. Except for a few privately owned houses, most housing stock in the neighborhood was managed by the municipal housing bureau, which moved workers and their families from other *danwei* to live here because their *danwei* could not provide them with housing. The neighborhood soon became overcrowded, with every single-family house shared by 20 to 30 families. Families built balconies and other kinds of extensions to increase living space as much as they could. Due to the high density and cost of relocation, the neighborhood was bypassed again by the government-led urban renewal programs and by private developers in the 1980s and 1990s. In the early 2000s, more than 4,000 people lived in an area of no more than 8 hectares. As the living conditions have worsened, those families who could afford to move have all left and rented their space out to migrant workers attracted to the central location of the place. The ones staying behind are mostly older people, laid-off workers, the unemployed, and the working poor. At the time of Liu and Wu's study in the mid-2000s, the highest household income of the families did not exceed 240 USD per month, and the majority earned only about half of that.

Similar old inner-city neighborhoods of high poverty can be found in many other cities across the country. Often sandwiched between modern skyscrapers and close to Central Business Districts, these low-rise inner-city neighborhoods house a mixture of migrant workers and impoverished long-term residents.

Degraded workers' villages

The second type of poverty neighborhood is the degraded work-unit housing compound. SOE reforms have produced a large number of laid-off workers with no prospect of re-employment. Unable to afford commercial housing, the laid-off workers and their families have stayed in work-unit compounds. In these places too there is a mixture of homeownership arrangements. Some sitting tenants have purchased their apartments from the work-units at deeply discounted prices; some have only partial ownership rights; and some have no ownership rights at all and remain as tenants of public rental housing. Due to the high unemployment rates, low income, and lack of maintenance, many remaining work-unit compounds have lost their former glory and become poverty neighborhoods.

In July 2011, I visited one of such workers' villages in a factory compound in the city of Harbin. During its peak days in the 1960s, the factory employed more than 20,000 workers and its housing compounds bustled with life. By 2011, the workforce of the factory had shrunk to little more than 2,000. The factory sold a large portion of its land holdings to private developers. Some apartment buildings have been demolished and replaced by high-rise commercial apartments and shopping malls. In the remaining housing quarters live a large number of aging and unemployed workers and their families. While taking a walk in the workers' village, I spotted a few fading images of Chairman Mao and other national leaders painted on the walls of some residential buildings, telling of the place's glorious past that is now long gone.

Liu and Wu (2006) examined the poverty condition in another workers' village in Nanjing, which was built in the 1970s to house the returnee population from the Cultural Revolution. The workers' village is composed of more than 50 apartment buildings, most of which are of low-quality construction and lack private kitchens and toilets. The local government assigned jobs for the returnees in collectively owned enterprises and promised better housing arrangements after the transition. But the promise was not delivered – more than two decades have passed and residents still live in the same apartment blocks, including dilapidated housing stocks, and now with their grown-up children. About 40 percent of the residents in the village were unemployed, and 65 percent of households earned less than 120 USD per month.

Minimum living

To address the new urban poverty, the central government has expanded the Minimum Living Standard Program (MLSP), also called *dibao* – meaning "protecting low-income families." A large proportion of MLSP recipients are concentrated in the old inner-city neighborhoods and work-unit housing compounds. Established in 1993, the subsidy is intended to make up the gap between the recipient's income and the official poverty line. The funding initially came from the Ministry of Finance but over the years the program has relied more on local contributions. By 1999, more than 500 cities had already enrolled in the program (Solinger, 2006). There is no universal MLSP standard across the country, and every city can decide on its own standards and procedures. The number of recipients of MLSP support increased from 4 million in 2001, to 12.35 million in 2002, and to 69 million in 2009 (Chen, Gu, and Wu, 2006; He et al., 2010). In 2010, the average MLSP aid was 221 RMB per person per month for urban residents and 96 RMB for rural residents (Wu, 2010b). These are telling figures – even for the minimum cost of living, there are separate standards for urban and rural residents, and the MLSP standard for urban residents is more than double that for rural residents. Moreover, the amount of the subsidy, ranging between 15 and 32 USD per person per month, is far from enough to guarantee living at the minimum survival level, due to the high inflation and the rising costs of living. Chen, Gu and Wu (2006) note that only in a few of the largest cities, such as Shanghai and Beijing, have city governments devoted substantial funding to the MLSP, while in most other places, the program is much less effective as city governments are either reluctant or unable to spend on poverty alleviation.

The central government has experimented with a number of policies to pacify the discontents of the new urban poor (Solinger, 2006). In addition to the MLSP, the central government has also tried job creation programs for re-employment. But these programs are largely ineffective in helping laid-off and unemployed urban workers, since most private-sector jobs are taken either by migrant workers or the better educated. Special subsidies are also allocated to the areas hit hardest by SOE reforms, such as the three northeastern provinces. The central government has also been promoting the rule of law, trying to divert the discontented to the court system and prevent them from taking to the streets (Solinger, 2006). But, as with the MLSP, all these measures for tackling the rising poverty cannot reverse the larger trends of state retreat from social welfare provision, economic restructuring, and uneven development, which are the root causes of the new poverty.

CREATING WEALTH AND POVERTY THROUGH URBAN RENEWAL

One of the often-neglected causes of the increasing inequality is urban renewal and redevelopment. Beginning with Beijing and Shanghai in the early 1990s, cities in China have gone through similar cycles of demolition and construction, the process of which has generated an extremely wealthy class of real-estate developers and investors, an affluent class of managers and professionals in the property sector, and a vast number of residents falling into poverty as they are displaced without adequate compensation. Two high-profile developers and their projects – SOHO China in Beijing and Shui On Group, based in Shanghai – illustrate how wealth and poverty are produced in the redevelopment game.

SOHO China stands out in the pack of real-estate development companies in China for its extensive use of architecture for branding. The company began to build its reputation as "patron for contemporary architecture" – as it calls itself, with its Jianwai SOHO project in the Central Business District of Beijing. Since Jianwai SOHO, the company has invited a different international architecture firm to design each and every one of its two dozen projects in Beijing and Shanghai. Using star architects for branding is not unique to China, but the effects of using architecture to boost project sales are more spectacular in China than elsewhere, and this has to do with the extremely rushed cycle of building construction, the limited credit for private enterprises, and developers' heavy dependence on pre-sale revenues. The speed of construction is extremely fast in Chinese cities, especially in prime locations such as the Central Business District in Beijing. The period from architectural design to construction to sales is often less than a few months. In the case of Jianwai SOHO, the developers wanted to start construction as soon as possible and gave the architects only three months for the design of the whole project. Because of the lack of other channels to raise funds for construction, such as stock markets or bank mortgages, pre-sales and down payments from property buyers – often 20 to 30 percent of the total purchase price – are crucial for developers to maintain cash flow. If developers can generate enough buzz, then they can attract potential buyers and succeed in pre-sales. Toward this end, SOHO China often organizes extravagant parties and architectural design symposiums. Its publicity campaigns are so successful that the company can often finish selling all units even before anything is built. Pre-sales – sales of properties before the buildings are finished or even before anything is built – are risky for investors, and the use of star architects can help build investors' confidence and encourage their decision to invest. Jianwai SOHO targeted the group of people at the top of the income hierarchy. According to a report released by the company, in Jianwai SOHO's 2004 sales, there were 180 investors who bought more than 10 million USD worth of property per person (Ren, 2011).

During my fieldwork with the sales staff of SOHO China – most of whom were in their late twenties and early thirties – they proudly told me about their biggest deals and commissions. One of my interviewees, Ms Sun, revealed to me that her highest weekly commission was 170,000 RMB (about 24,300 USD) – several times what a well-paid urban professional in Beijing can make in a year. The concept-driven and design-intensive strategy has brought great commercial success to the company, made dozens of millionaires among its employees, and made the CEOs Pan Shiyi and Zhang Xin among the wealthiest private entrepreneurs in the country. In 2011, when the central government called for tightening bank credit for developers, Pan Shiyi told the media that his company would not have to worry about financing, since the company's current cash holdings of 19 billion RMB would be more than enough to finance its next projects (Ren, 2011).

While bottles of champagne were opened, ribbons were cut, and millionaires and billionaires were made, many ordinary residents lost their homes and relocated to the urban periphery, joining the army of the urban poor. The transformation of Xintiandi in Shanghai is an example of these parallel cycles. Before its redevelopment, the area of Xintiandi was made up of old residential row houses built before the 1930s. In 1996, Shanghai's Luwan district government signed an agreement with Shui On Group from Hong Kong to develop the Xintiandi area. The area covered 52 hectares of land and consisted of 23 residential neighborhoods with some 70,000 households and more than 800 work units. The developer provided capital and the government facilitated moving people out. In 1997, the developer decided to begin the project by building a brand-new park to change the scenery of the area, and, in 43 days, the local government helped to convince and, in some cases forced, 3,800 families and 156 work units to move out to make land available. Following the opening of the new park, the developer symbolically preserved two blocks of the original row houses, turned them into a pedestrian shopping street with brand-name shops, and demolished the rest of the neighborhood in order to build new commercial properties.

By the summer of 2006, when I revisited the place, Xintiandi had become the new center of Shanghai's night-life and the two pedestrian blocks were filled with bars, music, diners, and tourists. But the area surrounding Xintiandi was still in ruins, with old buildings torn down while new ones had not yet been built. Most residents had already taken compensation and moved out. In the first phase of the redevelopment, in 1997, every family received an average of about $15,600 – less than the commission from a single deal that Ms Sun made at SOHO China. The real-estate prices in Shanghai skyrocketed after 1998, and Shui On Group agreed to raise the compensation per family to $20,000, but still it was far from enough to purchase an apartment unit in the city. The families remaining in Xintiandi in 2006 were mostly lower-income residents living in extremely crowded conditions. They had not yet given up hope and were still trying to negotiate for better compensation. A Luwan district official told me that all the remaining residents would have to move out, even if they did not agree with the compensation, because the city had just decided to build a new subway stop in the area, which would be a "legitimate" reason to move people out – because this was a public project and therefore in the "public interest." When I visited the area again during the 2010 Shanghai World Expo, the half-demolished row houses and residents were all gone, and replaced by a brand-new subway stop, just as the Luwan official had said four years before.

In the media, one often reads news about *dingzihu* – residents who refuse to leave and in the end receive handsome compensation packages from developers and become rich. But, in reality, rich *dingzihu* belong to the minority, and the vast majority of displaced residents have been moved out of their homes with inadequate compensation and settled on the urban periphery. Between 1995 and 2008, more than 1 million households in Shanghai were relocated for various redevelopment projects – in most cases, without fair compensation (Ren, 2008b).

Redevelopment projects such as Xintiandi have become a new mechanism of generating poverty and inequality.

POPULAR PERCEPTIONS OF INEQUALITY

As seen in the previous sections, a large number of studies have been conducted to examine the causes and patterns of inequality in China today, measured in Gini coefficient, income gaps, and differential access to education, housing, and good jobs across social groups. But what is little known is the popular reaction to the high levels of inequality and distributional injustice. In other words, what do Chinese citizens think about the unequal society they are living in?

In 2004, sociologist Martin K. Whyte conducted one of the first surveys of Chinese popular attitudes toward inequality trends, drawing on a sample of more than 3,000 respondents aged between 18 and 70 in both rural and urban areas. The survey delivered some quite perplexing results, many of which contradict the popular contention of what Whyte (2011) calls "the social volcano scenario" – i.e., that high inequality leads to vast discontent and eventually large-scale popular protests will break out and overthrow one-party rule. The larger picture emerging from the survey is that the average Chinese citizen is quite accepting and even positive rather than angry or bitter about current inequalities. The majority of the respondents agreed that differences in ability and talents explain who is rich (69.5 percent) and who is poor (61.3 percent), and 62.8 percent thought that people should be allowed to keep what they earn even if it leads to inequality. On the other hand, only 27 percent believed that the unfairness of the economic system has a large influence on who is rich, and only 29.5 percent supported redistribution of wealth from the rich to the poor. In short, the survey shows that the Chinese are very accepting about inequalities. There is little sign of perceived injustice, or nostalgia for the socialist years. What is even more surprising is the different perception of inequality between rural and urban populations. Considering the gap in income and living standards between rural and urban areas, one would assume that Chinese peasants have more resentment toward injustice than their urban counterparts. But the 2004 survey shows that "rural people in general, and farmers in particular, express more accepting or positive views than others about current inequalities and show less enthusiasm for government redistribution, despite their low relative social status" (Whyte, 2011: 279). Urban residents, especially the well educated, well connected, and well resourced, tend to express more critical attitudes toward inequalities and are more in favor of redistribution.

The general pattern of acceptance toward inequality across the urban–rural divide has to be understood in the larger context of market transition and the open mobility it created. In the socialist decades, individuals were locked in different cells – work units, rural production teams, and people's communes. Despite there being a high degree of equality *within* these cells, resources and life chances were unequally distributed across the cells, and people had little chance to change their fate based on hard work and talent. The market reform dismantled these cells and created an open mobility structure – rural people were no longer confined to farming and urban residents to their *danwei* (Whyte, 2011). Thus, the general positive attitude, argued by Whyte, has to be understood in light of the contrast between the socialist years and the market-reform era.

As for the question of why urban residents are more critical of inequality than their rural counterparts, a number of different explanations are possible. Whyte (2011) argues that this reflects the loss of the privileges they experienced in the socialist years. In addition, it might also be that rural residents lack information about and visual exposure to the extreme wealth that those living in cities see regularly, such as expensive cars, extravagant mansions, upmarket hotels and restaurants, and luxury consumer goods. In 2011, a 20-year-old girl named Guo Meimei caused a major controversy on the Internet, after showing off her wealth on *weibo* by posting pictures of villas, Hermes bags, and a Maserati car. Her micro-blog had millions of hits within a few days and her showing-off angered many of China's urban netizens. Reporters followed her everywhere, and eventually she appeared on TV to apologize – about her false claim that she is a manager for the Red Cross Society. She fled the country a few months later.[2] The Guo Meimei incident illustrates two points in line with our discussion here: first, urban Chinese are more sensitive and critical of inequality than rural people because they have more information and exposure to inequality; second, although inequality and extreme wealth are tolerated in China today, they continue to be triggers and targets for popular discontent.

CONCLUSIONS

This chapter has examined the increasing social and spatial inequality in Chinese cities resulting from economic restructuring, the changing welfare regime, and large-scale urban renewal. In terms of social inequality, research has shown that the gender and education gaps in income have widened in the process of market reform, with rural women being the most disadvantaged group in educational achievement and earnings. Research has also shown that categorical variables such as city of residence or employment sector matter as much as individual attributes, and there is relatively high egalitarianism within social groups and increasing inequality between groups. In terms of the spatial distribution of poverty, geographers have identified three types of high-poverty neighborhoods – old inner-city areas, degraded work-unit housing compounds, and migrant villages – with the first type being the most destitute due to housing a large number of the unemployed. Although the national level of absolute poverty has dropped, a growing urban underclass of the unemployed, the working poor, and migrants has emerged. The divide between the property-owning and propertyless classes has grown bigger and bigger, as property such as housing becomes one of the most important assets for generating return on investment. Urban restructuring has further exacerbated social stratification. As a small number of developers, investors, and professionals in the real-estate sector have become extremely wealthy, profiting so much from the property bubble that few want to see it end, a large number of residents have lost their homes and been relocated to the urban periphery. The popular attitudes toward inequality have shown surprisingly high levels of acceptance, however, due to improved standards of living and the open mobility structure brought by the market reform across the rural–urban divide.

The current configuration of inequality is likely to change in the very near future. In the next decade, we may witness more within-group inequality than before, as individual attributes are rewarded differentially. With regard to spatial concentrations of inequality, some of the current poverty neighborhoods may disappear as redevelopment touches more and more places, and the urban poor may move further away from the city center and form new pockets of poverty on the urban edge. Lastly, large-scale demolition and displacement as in the 1990s are probably unlikely to continue, as the central government passes new regulations to forbid such practices in order to ensure social stability. Urban renewal may be less of a factor in creating wealth and poverty in the future, but the past two decades of urban redevelopment have already significantly changed the socio-spatial structures of Chinese cities, and their impact will be felt for generations to come.

6 | Cultural Economy ─────────────

Compared to the socialist period, when personal consumption choices were limited and cultural production was under strict control by the state, the market reform gave birth to a vibrant urban cultural scene. The opportunities for consumption have greatly diversified and the state control over cultural production has relaxed. After 30 years of breakneck growth, the Chinese city is a place of creativity, opulence, conspicuous consumption, but also sharp inequality. Urban residents enjoy an unprecedented variety of choices of consumer goods and services, provided by domestic and multinational companies vying for China's huge consumer market. International luxury brands compete with one another to open stores in China, targeting the affluent upper-middle class. City governments have poured tremendous amounts of capital into building cultural facilities, such as museums, opera houses, exhibition centers, stadia, and libraries (Denton, 2005). The number of museums, for example, had reached more than 3,000 by 2009, and most of these were built after 2000 (Zhang, 2011). Chinese cities have also become hotbeds of urban pop culture, and dynamic developments are taking place in music, film, and visual and performance art. New cultural elites have emerged in the course of the development of the urban cultural economy, such as writers, artists, celebrities, film directors, architects, and designers, and they are the gatekeepers and tastemakers in the new cultural marketplace. The local and translocal cultural elites mingle easily with the business elites. It is common, for example, for Chinese real-estate tycoons to include a gallery or an art museum in their buildings for place-branding and to invite independent film-makers to make promotional video clips. The boundaries between high culture, low culture, and commerce have blurred, and cultural and economic capital have become easily interchangeable.

It is beyond the scope of this chapter to survey the entire field of the urban cultural scene, and I choose to focus on three cultural milieus to explore how marketization, globalization, and new forms of state intervention have together reshaped the dynamics of the cultural economy. The three milieus are urban consumption, nightlife, and arts districts. I examine the specific sites where new practices of consumption, nightlife, and cultural production take place, such as individual homes, restaurants, bars, clubs, and arts districts. The first section uses an anecdote to illustrate the lifestyles of the Chinese middle class, which is still small in numbers but nevertheless is the driving force for cultural industries. The second section, on consumption, examines how individuals experience both freedom and disempowerment in China's consumerist revolution. The third section, on nightlife, discusses the evolution and the changing geography of Shanghai's club scene, as organically developed nightlife venues were cracked down on by the government and replaced by state-sponsored flagship nightlife districts such as Xintiandi and the Bund. Compared to the fields of shopping, where there is little state control, and nightlife districts, where moderate levels of state intervention can be observed, new arts districts are developed primarily to promote cultural industries and are places where deliberate state planning and surveillance are clearly on display. Although the degree of state control, globalization, and marketization varies across cultural economic sectors, it will become clear from the following sections that culture, whether as leisure or as capital (Wang, 2004), has become a site for new forms of state and market intervention and exhibits different gender, racial, and class dynamics today than in the past.

THE URBAN MIDDLE CLASS

Ms Zhang is one of the friends I see every time I am back in Beijing. In her early thirties now, she has worked for a number of international and local high-tech firms as a marketing executive and earns a competitive salary that enables her to live a privileged life in the city. In the early 2000s, she worked for a software company in Zhongguancun, the high-tech district in the northwest part of Beijing that has a large concentration of universities and start-up companies. She lived in a two-bedroom rental apartment in a large residential complex near the North Fifth Ring Road, from which she could easily commute to work every morning by train. The apartment was comfortably decorated, with large walk-in closets, smooth floor tiles, and all the modern entertainment equipment. Compared to the housing conditions of her parents' generation – many still live in one-bedroom apartments packed with old furniture accumulated over the years – Ms Zhang's apartment was spacious, and had a modern and minimalist touch. When I visited we would go to the many small and independently owned boutiques in the city, buy clothes from local designers, and, in the evenings, sample the restaurants, bars, and clubs in the Sanlitun area – Beijing's premier nightlife district.

In the mid-2000s Ms Zhang got married. Her husband has a master's degree in engineering from the US and works for an American high-tech company in Beijing; the two of them met through work. With two competitive salaries and help from his parents, who are retired high-ranking government officials, the couple moved into an upper-middle-class residential complex near the Olympic Park. Her new apartment was meticulously decorated, looking like a model room from a sleek design magazine. We sat on her large Italian sofa in the middle of the living room and watched her wedding DVD. The execution of the wedding was complete with Chinese urban middle-class desires – white tablecloths, green lawns, a custom-made wedding gown, make-up artists, flower petals, flowing champagne, and the ceremony of exchanging wedding rings in front of guests, which is a new custom recently adopted in Chinese weddings.

We still went out shopping and checked out new restaurants in Beijing, but by 2007 the shopping and entertainment scene in Beijing had changed. Small and independent stores had become harder and harder to find, and many of the coffee shops, restaurants, and clubs in the Sanlitun area had been demolished and replaced by gigantic shopping complexes housing global brands such as Adidas, Muji, Apple, and Starbucks. The excitement of hunting for local designer labels was gone, and shopping in Beijing had become predictable and familiar, just like shopping in some parts of New York or Hong Kong. But Ms Zhang was not especially concerned about the changes, and her wardrobe had already begun to internationalize with global designer labels such as Marc Jacobs and Jimmy Choo.

Tired of the high-intensity work schedule of 70 hours per week plus meetings on weekends, which is normal in the competitive high-tech sector in Beijing, Ms Zhang changed her job. Now she works for a Swedish outdoor-clothing company that just opened an office in Beijing, and for no more than 40 hours a week. Her shopping and dining habitat in the city has changed too. Probably influenced by her Swedish colleagues, Ms Zhang is now very much into the outdoors, fitness, and organic foods. When I saw her last time in her Jianwai SOHO office, high heels and designer business suits were gone and she was wearing a soft cotton blouse and yoga pants. We had dinner in a newly opened organic café and, over dinner, from time to time she would play with her brand-new iPhone 4.

There are many urbanites like Ms Zhang – young, educated, English-speaking, career-oriented, technology-savvy – who have enough disposable income to acquire the latest gadgets and take advantage of the endless cultural offerings in large cities like Beijing. They live a lifestyle not that dissimilar from their counterparts in other global cities, and they contrast sharply with the older generation of their parents, workers, and peasants. The Chinese middle class is a broad social group and it is defined as much by cultural capital, political orientation, and consumption preference as by income (Goodman, 2008; Anagnost, 2008). If measured by consumption capacity, for example, households with daily expenditure between 10 and 100 US dollars in purchase parity terms, about 12 percent of the Chinese population falls into the category of the middle class (Kharas, 2010). The Chinese urban middle class, although still a minority in numbers, is the driving force behind and the target group of the emerging cultural industries.

CONSUMPTION: FREEDOM, HIERARCHY, AND INEQUALITY

Consumption is one of the urban cultural milieus where the state exerts little control. In contrast to the scarcity of the socialist era, contemporary Chinese cities are consumer societies of abundance. Every street and block is lined with supermarkets, convenience stores, bakeries, boutiques, and restaurants catering to different budgets and tastes. The urban consumer culture in China today is characterized by vastly expanded choices for personal differentiation and greater control by citizens over their private lives. Davis (2005) documents these trends vividly in her study of urban middle-class families in Shanghai in the mid-2000s. She observes the tremendous sense of freedom felt by urban residents through the experience of consumption, especially when the residents recall the past material scarcity and political suppression under socialism. With the privatization of housing, for the first time since the 1950s, urban Chinese now can own their homes, and many of them invest their life savings and creative energies in decorating their new apartments. Davis visited the giant IKEA store in Shanghai and witnessed how the Swedish furniture chain became an instant hit among middle-class Chinese desiring a modern and sophisticated home. It is common for developers to sell unfurnished apartment units, and homeowners need to do everything by themselves to transform a concrete bunker into a comfortable home. Home decoration has thus become a multibillion-dollar industry, and Chinese urbanites derive a strong sense of freedom and empowerment from creating their private paradise (Davis, 2005; Zhang, 2010).

On the Internet, new homeowners actively exchange ideas and information on home maintenance and decor – from how to stop bathroom leaks, install a new kitchen, or rewire the electrical system, to where to get floor tiles in the latest fashion at group discount prices. Home-decor magazines have also flourished, featuring the hottest Scandinavian designers, which further fire up middle-class desire and also help shape market trends and consumer tastes. Home decor has also become a site for conspicuous consumption, and China's nouveau riche seek distinction and display their wealth by lavishly decorating their homes with furniture made in Europe – although many European brands are found to be counterfeit and manufactured locally.[1]

Fine dining is another field where distinction and status are actively sought by local and translocal elites. Culture sociologist James Farrer has documented how haute cuisine arrived in Shanghai after 2000, with international star chefs opening new restaurants in renovated historical mansions from the colonial era (Farrer, 2010a). In the 1980s, Western restaurants gradually appeared in Shanghai, but mostly they were located in international hotels and targeted foreign businessmen and tourists. Australian owner Michelle Gaunaut opened Shanghai's first fine Western dining venue, M on the Bund, in 1998 in a 1920s building on the Bund. With a spectacular view of the futuristic skyline of Pudong, M was an immediate hit, attracting international travelers, returnees, and wealthy local Chinese. Following M's success, Bund

Three, an upmarket dining, shopping, and entertainment venue, opened in another historical building on the Bund in 2003. The renovation of the building alone cost 80 million USD, and the tenants are restricted to the most prestigious – such as a venture by the star chef Jean-Georges Vongerichten – in order to mark the status of the property and distinguish it from competitors. Farrer (2010a) observes that the new upmarket dining scene in Shanghai exhibits a particular geography: old colonial buildings in the former French and international concessions are actively sought after by international star chefs and are lavishly renovated to house the most exclusive dining and entertainment venues for the transnational capitalist elite. Star chefs often circulate among global cities – Tokyo, New York, Paris, Hong Kong – to build their careers, and they create similar exclusive and upmarket spaces of haute cuisine in each city; their outposts in Shanghai integrate the city into the global network of culinary distinction. The Shanghai city government is very much aware of the cultural capital created by star chefs and their restaurants and is highly supportive of the emerging international dining establishments in the city (Farrer, 2010a).

Urban consumption, as in the forms of shopping, home decor, and upmarket dining, offers a lens through which to observe not only the unprecedented freedom of choice that Chinese urbanites enjoy today, but also the rising inequality between the haves and have-nots. While the urban middle class are energized by decorating their private homes and the transnational elites are dining in the exclusive restaurants on the Bund, the millions of urban poor are barely surviving at the margin of the glamorous new urban China. Urban consumption does offer a sense of freedom, but as Chinese urban society becomes more unequal and the gap between the rich and the poor continues to widen, consumption has also become a site of disempowerment and alienation, as consumer citizenship ultimately rests upon the ability to pay.

NIGHTLIFE: FROM ORGANICALLY GROWN
AND STATE-PLANNED

A vibrant urban nightlife scene has come back after the three decades of socialism, with the rising disposable income, massive capital investments into nightlife establishments, and Chinese cities' increasing integration into the global cultural economy. In large metropolises, tens of thousands of restaurants, bars, clubs, and live music venues have appeared, catering to different budgets and tastes. From the 1980s to the present, the development of nightlife in urban China has gone through several distinct phases, from the emergence of a small number of bars in international hotels in the 1980s, to government crackdowns on independent clubs in the late 1990s, and to active promotion and planning of nightlife districts by local governments since the 2000s (Zeng, 2010; Chew, 2010; Farrer, 2010b).

Shanghai is known for its glamorous and decadent nightlife in the colonial era. Although the trendy clubs and their international clientele in today's Shanghai remind one of the city's past, the gender and racial dynamics of Shanghai nightlife today are very different (Farrer and Field, 2012). Cultural historian Andrew Field documents that, between the 1910s and 1930s, under the influence of the Jazz Age, the city was filled with dance halls and cabaret venues, where Chinese mingled with Westerners on the dance floor (Field, 2010). In "taxi dance halls," young Chinese women recruited from the provinces worked as entertainers and hostesses, and male customers paid to dance with these *wunu* (i.e., dancing girls). Many of the *wunu* developed relationships with their wealthy male patrons outside the dance halls, and became their wives and lovers (Farrer and Field, 2012). There were also obvious racial hierarchies in the nightlife spaces of old Shanghai, with Westerners occupying superior positions to the locals. Comparing the Republican and the post-reform periods, Farrer and Field (2012) note two major changes in gender and racial relations in Shanghai's nightlife. First,

Chinese and Westerners, male and female, now have more equal social footing than in the 1930s. The second and most notable change, they argue, is the growing presence of highly educated, English-speaking, white-collar Chinese women, who have changed the demography of the Shanghai nightlife scene. By frequenting nightlife venues, these Chinese women become familiar with both Chinese and Western forms of sociability. Compared to the early twentieth century, distinctions in nightlife are based less on racial, ethnic, and gender divides and more on "cultural capital," in the forms of language skills, education, overseas exposure, and familiarity with foreign culture.

The geography of Shanghai nightlife has also changed over time. Beginning in the 1980s, with the market reform, discos, bars, and clubs gradually came back, first reappearing in international hotels catering to foreign tourists and business travelers. According to Farrer (2010b), the first disco for foreigners in Shanghai opened in 1988 in the Jinjiang Hotel and, in 1994, Judy's opened, an independent club owned by a Shanghainese woman who called herself Judy and her German boyfriend. Judy's had close connections with the police department of the Luwan district government, and its first location was in the basement of the Armed Police Conference Hall on Fuming Road. The club attracted a mixed crowd of foreign businessmen, foreign students, prostitutes, and local Shanghainese seeking interactions with foreigners. In 1996, Judy's moved to Maoming Road, a leafy and quiet residential street in the former French concession. Other bars and clubs followed, and Maoming Road became the nightlife quarter of Shanghai in the late 1990s. Below is a picture of a Friday night on this bar street right before the government shut it down.

This nocturnal panorama included the fashionable and sexily dressed bar customers, prostitutes accosting middle-aged foreign visitors, rural children aggressively selling flowers, and beggars mobbing taxis arriving at the bars. Exasperated policemen stopped fights, tried to control street prostitution, and urged on traffic. (Farrer, 2011: 752)

The city government of Shanghai shut down the bars on Maoming Road in 2000, citing concerns over crime, drugs, prostitution, sanitation, noise, and disturbance to residents. There was widespread speculation that many retired officials living in the vicinity complained about the noise from the bars and clubs, and urged the city government to close the bar street. Regardless of the speculation, the government stance toward nightlife in the 1990s was largely hostile. Local governments associated the organically developed bar streets with vice and crime and decided that they had to be "sanitized."

Nightlife in Shanghai did not disappear after the government crackdown, but it has assumed a new geography, having been directed to government-promoted nightlife districts. After 2000, Xintiandi became one of the most upmarket nightlife districts in Shanghai (Ren, 2008b). It is a textbook example of a high-end, sanitized nightlife district with strong government endorsement. Before the redevelopment by Shui On Group, the area of Xintiandi consisted of dilapidated row houses. At one corner of Xintiandi is the Communist Party Hall. Just 80 years ago, Mao Zedong and his 13 comrades held the first meeting of the Chinese Communist Party there. As the birthplace of the CCP, the old Party Hall is listed as a national landmark and cannot be demolished. The developer and architects kept two blocks of row houses near the old Party Hall. On the north block, most of the original buildings were retained. The facades of the old houses were repaired, and the original color and texture were restored. The interior space was gut-renovated by Shanghai's best interior design firms. The slate-gray bricks and stones from old residences were used for new construction and as paving material for pedestrian streets. The heavy wooden gates were replaced with glass storefronts displaying brand-name luxury goods.

On the south block, a modern shopping and entertainment complex replaced old row houses.

Shui On carefully handpicked the tenants for Xintiandi. Among the tenants in the renovated buildings, the majority are upmarket restaurants, bars, nightclubs, coffee shops, boutiques, and commercial galleries. The rest include boutique hotels, beauty spas, and a cinema complex. Although the price range of these shops is out of reach for many Shanghainese, the growing population of foreign expatriates and wealthy Chinese has brought a steady supply of consumers to the high-end shops at Xintiandi. It is a must-see destination for foreign business travelers, and the bars and clubs at Xintiandi are filled night after night by conference-goers and businessmen on company expense accounts. Xintiandi has become a tourist mecca for domestic visitors as well. About 30,000 people stroll through its shops on a daily basis, and according to Shui On's estimates, about 70 percent of these visitors are Chinese. Xintiandi symbolizes how Shanghai has been increasingly integrated into the global economy and how new consumption patterns have been generated as a result of locals adapting to global cultural traits. For example, until recently, restaurants in China did not have outdoor cafes. However, the sidewalk cafes at Xintiandi are even more popular than places with indoor tables, because the theatricality created by the spatial design makes Xintiandi Square a place to people-watch and to be seen (Ren, 2008b).

Farrer (2011) correctly observes that conspicuous consumption and nightlife are no longer considered politically dangerous and morally corrupt in these government-backed entertainment districts. Compared to its unruly bar streets in the 1990s, Shanghai's new nightlife venues are clean, sanitized, and closely monitored. Street prostitution has disappeared at Xintiandi thanks to a private security team working exclusively there (Farrer, 2011). Xintiandi has become a role model for state-backed flagship projects across the country, and clones of Xintiandi have already appeared in a score of other cities.

ARTS DISTRICTS AND CULTURAL INDUSTRIES

Artist quarters in Beijing tend to form in rural villages on the urban periphery. The ambiguous jurisdictional organization and loose land regulation have made urban fringes attractive places for artists to settle. In the short period since 2000, many artist villages have appeared at the urban–rural intersections in Beijing, triggering a further migration of international galleries and a construction boom on the periphery. Beginning with 798 Factory (see chapter 3), some of the artist villages have been turned into official arts districts by the city government. The districtification of former artist villages indicates the state's interest in promoting cultural industries while maintaining control over cultural production.

The enthusiastic government support for cultural industries in China is largely driven by the desire of the national government to promote Chinese culture and to build "soft power," and by the attempts of both the national and local governments to upgrade from labor-intensive manufacturing to knowledge-based industries. Joseph Nye (2005) argues that instead of hard power such as military and economic strength, China is competing with the US by building soft sources of power such as culture, political values, and diplomacy. Nye (2005) also points out that China's soft power still has a long way to go to match that of the US; for example, China does not have cultural industries like Hollywood. Policymakers in China are very much aware of the imbalance in the cultural trade and view the development of cultural industries as the right path to build China's soft power. The widespread support for cultural industries also reflects the urgency felt by the national and local governments for economic upgrading. The tenth National Five-Year Plan (2001–5) stated that the rationale for promoting "cultural industries with Chinese characteristics" is to stimulate domestic consumption demand, increase employment opportunities, and restructure the national economy

(State Council, 2001). As Keane (2006, 2007) rightly points out, cultural industries have become a "super-sign" in China, invested with supernatural powers to transform and revitalize the urban economy. For many Chinese cities trying to move up the value chain of global production, developing cultural industries is viewed as the solution to make the leap from "Made in China" to "Created in China" and to achieve many goals at once, such as wealth creation, the reuse of traditional resources, green production, talent renewal, and industrial upgrading. It is within this context that arts districts in Beijing and other large cities have flourished.

Transient art space

Beijing's arts districts on the periphery are inevitably transient in nature. As real-estate development continuously encroaches on the rural hinterland, the urban–rural intersection is in a constant state of flux. The more than 20 artist clusters on the city's periphery have met varying fates of development – from crackdowns by governments, to evictions of artists by developers, to official recognition and endorsement. The different trajectories of artist villages depend on the attitude of the city and district governments – only when the governments recognize the economic potential of artist clusters and consequently endorse them can these villages avoid demolition and disbandment. The earliest artist cluster in Beijing was Yuanmingyuan artist village (1984–95), formed in the northwest edge of the city. Having started in the mid-1980s, Yuanmingyuan attracted over 300 migrant artists from all over the country in the early 1990s. Many of these artists had quit stable jobs in cultural institutions in the public sector and come to Beijing to pursue an alternative career. But in the aftermath of the Tiananmen student movement of 1989, the political climate in Beijing was conservative and the city authorities had an attitude of deep mistrust toward artists. The public security bureau viewed the artist congregation at Yuanmingyuan as a potential social threat and, in 1995, Haidian district police shut down the village and evicted all artists.

After Yuanmingyuan, 798 Factory emerged as the central art district in Beijing, in the midst of a booming urban economy and relaxed political control (see chapter 3). But the rising rents at 798 soon pushed out most resident artists to other villages further away from the city center. The émigrés from Yuanmingyuan and 798, together with newcomers, soon formed other artist villages in the Chaoyang and Tongzhou districts on the northeast edge of Beijing. However, as property development intensified on the periphery, some of these new clusters, such as Suojia village and Feijia village in Chaoyang district, soon met the same fate of demolition and eviction that confronted many other urban neighborhoods. With the success of the 798 art district, the Chaoyang district government has no interest in preserving other artist clusters and instead intends to develop the peripheral land for other high-value-added service industries. The various trajectories of artist villages indicate the transient nature of art spaces in Beijing and the crucial role of the local state – at both the city and district levels – in determining their preservation and survival.

The Rise of Songzhuang

Unlike 798 Factory, which has become gentrified by international galleries and boutique shops catering to tourists, Songzhuang town remains a primary site of artistic production and was home to about 3,000 artists by 2009. Songzhuang town is located 28 kilometers east of the Beijing city center in Tongzhou district, and it was designated in 2006 as one of the first 11 Cultural and Creative Industry (CCI) Clusters of Beijing – special development zones concentrating enterprises in cultural industries such as design, publishing, advertising, performance art, animation, music, and film production. The population of Songzhuang town is about 100,000 residents, 60 percent of whom are villagers and 40 percent temporary residents – the latter consisting mostly of migrant workers but also including artists. Among the 47 natural villages in Songzhuang, 22 currently have artist studios and galleries, and 80 percent of the artists live in Xiaopu village, the place where a dozen artists expelled from Yuanmingyuan first resettled. In spite of pressure from the city police, the head of Xiaopu village, Cui Dabai, allowed the artists to stay, but primarily for economic reasons. Compared to other villages, the farmland of Xiaopu village is less fertile for agricultural crops, and villagers have a lower average income. A farmer in the early 1990s in Xiaopu village could only make 300 RMB at most in a good year, but by renting space to artists, villagers could collect 1,000–2,000 RMB per year. Some artists also offered to pay up to 5,000 RMB to buy courtyard houses from villagers; this was considered a fortune in the early 1990s, so the village committee even encouraged villagers to lease land to artists. As the village head, Mr Cui, commented in an interview, "I just wanted our villagers to have more income. It's not against the Party or Socialism. What's wrong with that?"[2] The artists' need for a new place to settle after the crackdown on Yuanmingyuan thus converged with the villagers' interest in generating more income. Songzhuang, the largest artist village in Beijing, was born at this unique juncture of time and space.

The artist population in Songzhuang is diverse and highly stratified, ranging from rags-to-riches international auction stars to starving artists struggling to make a living on the city's edge. The top stratum consists of a small number of extremely wealthy and internationally known artists who have sold works at overseas auctions. The middle stratum includes the long-term resident artists who make a stable living by selling their works. The lower stratum, representing the majority of Songzhuang artists, is mostly made up of art-school graduates coming to Beijing from the provinces to seek more opportunities. This last group forms a sizable "creative underclass" of people without stable income who have difficulty making ends meet. About 40 percent of Songzhuang artists rent space from villagers, 50 percent rent studio space in former village factories, and only about 10 percent – the commercially successful minority – have built large studios on land leased from villagers. In spite of the large number of artists, there have yet to emerge any grassroots associations organized by artists, and socialization among the artists mostly takes place on an individual basis.

The rise of Songzhuang as a primary artist cluster in Beijing also needs to be situated in the broader context of the international art-market boom and China's real-estate development fever. In 2005, several works by contemporary Chinese artists were sold for record prices at Sotheby's and Christies' auctions, and since then contemporary Chinese art has become a financial instrument for speculation. The average auction prices of Chinese contemporary art doubled from 2002 to 2007. In 2002, there was only one Chinese artist on Sotheby's list of "rich young artists" – those born after 1950 with a single art auction sale of over 1 million US dollars – but by 2008, 34 Chinese artists appeared on the list (Zhao, 2007). The boom of contemporary Chinese art is part of the larger trend of the structural expansion of the international art market, which has witnessed an increasing number of art collectors and investors coming from emerging economies. New patrons from China and Southeast Asia have purchased many works by Chinese artists at overseas auctions.

Many of the internationally famous Chinese artists are based in Songzhuang and have poured their new wealth into the construction of large studios and gated residences in the village. In addition to such self-construction projects by affluent artists, fueled by money from overseas auctions, Songzhuang has witnessed a larger real-estate boom led by both private and public actors with the construction of residences, studios, museums, galleries, and large-scale infrastructure works. The investments in these projects come from diverse sources, including subsidies allocated by the city and district governments, funding from village governments, and the private capital of village entrepreneurs. The Beijing city government has allocated special funds to facilitate the development of the Songzhuang Cultural and Creative Industry Cluster. According to the ambitious district master plan, Songzhuang is part of the larger creative industry base for the development of the visual arts, animation, movie, and media sectors. By 2015, agricultural land in all villages in Songzhuang will be converted for urban residential and commercial uses, with the initial investment provided by the city government. In addition to this government-funded development, Xiaopu village has invested in its own construction projects, such as converting an abandoned bomb shelter into a cluster of studios and building a brand-new Songzhuang art museum and a boutique art station. Furthermore, individual entrepreneurs have also emerged, mostly farmers-turned-landlords, who have torn down their former one-story houses to build multi-story buildings or even bigger art complexes for leasing to artists. These real-estate developments have led to drastic transformations of the rural landscape.

Creative control of arts districts

The districtification of artist villages has also introduced new mechanisms of control and surveillance into the formerly under-regulated urban periphery. A number of organizations play a key role in the governing of arts districts, such as management offices set up by district governments, enterprises established by town and village governments (TVEs) to develop real estate and attract investment, government-sponsored civic associations mediating between artists and local governments, and, finally, village committees – the lowest level of China's administrative hierarchy – which represent individual villager-leaseholders and participate in decision-making on land development. Aside from village committees, the other three types of organizations are all state agencies newly added to monitor the operation of art districts. A small group of party officials, mostly appointed by the district government, dominate the executive boards of all these organizations. This interlocking organizational feature enables exclusive and concerted decision-making over land development and constitutes a new mode of state control over cultural production.

The control and surveillance by the government can be clearly observed in the management of the annual art festival in Songzhuang. Key officials from the town government directly participate in the organization and scrutiny of the festival. The management office first submits a proposal to the town government, which must be approved personally by the Party Secretary of Songzhuang. Then the proposal is sent to the upper level of the district government and reviewed by the Propaganda Department, the Culture Committee, and the Public Security Bureau. The district government also sends its own personnel to Songzhuang to check the actual artwork to be displayed, and the final decisions on what to include and exclude often depend on ambiguous moral judgments by individual officials.

While monitoring artist activities and annual art festivals, the town and village governments are also actively involved in property development through their satellite TVEs. Both the management office and Xiaopu village have set up their own business firms, the main role of which is to acquire land from villagers and to prepare the land for the next phase of real-estate development. The officials of the management office and village committee are also the executives of these TVEs. This arrangement is widely referred to as "one team of people, working under two titles." When they need to provide a government function – such as granting approvals for specific projects – the officials will represent the government, and when they need to perform a market-related function – such as acquiring and leasing land – the same people will represent business interests through the operation of their TVEs. As extensions of the local governments, the TVEs have monopoly power over land acquisition. With funds from the city government, bank loans, and private capital, the TVEs first undertake demolition and construction of infrastructure and then attract industries with subsidized land in hopes of generating more tax revenues. After the land value rises with the development, the TVEs will auction some of the land to private developers to collect land-leasing fees. Land acquisition often involves complex negotiations between village committees and the town government, and the results vary greatly depending on the power balance between the two. Because of the strong leadership of Mr Cui, Xiaopu village is the only village in Songzhuang that will not be demolished for the development of the cultural and creative industries cluster. Xiaopu village has formed its own TVE, and Mr Cui serves as its executive to ensure that the village can benefit from land development. Villagers are shareholders and receive a small amount of annual dividends from land-leasing fees. Other villages in Songzhuang with fewer resources and less negotiating power will be demolished and their land transferred to the city government.

The future of arts districts

The rampant property speculation in the arts districts in Beijing raises intriguing questions about the future development of cultural industries in China. For instance, can these arts districts, endorsed by the government, provide a new space for artistic production and an institutional platform for China's emerging cultural industries? Or are these just new instruments for the public–private coalition to reap profits from land speculation? These further lead to a larger question – can creative cities be made, and what does it take for a creative milieu to emerge? Beijing is by all means a magnet attracting creative talents from both within and outside China. With the accumulation of wealth, the rise of private art patrons, and the expansion of the international art market, a contemporary art scene has quickly flourished, and the creative drive has centered around the organic artist villages on the urban periphery. However, government intervention has quickly altered the cultural landscape of the city with the establishment of more than 20 Cultural and Creative Industry Clusters – and, in Shanghai, the number of such clusters had reached more than 75 by 2010. The districtification of artist villages is a new spatial strategy by the local state to control cultural production in the context of privatization and globalization. It is still too soon to determine whether or not the new state control will suffocate urban creativity. Creativity may migrate once again to new territories under the pressure of state surveillance and real-estate development fever, and artists and other creative types may confront, circumvent, and react to both state and market forces in their everyday production and resistance.

CONCLUSIONS

This chapter has provided some snapshots of the vibrant cultural economy emerging in Chinese cities, with specific attention paid to consumption, nightlife, and arts districts. Three larger trends can be observed as shaping the development of the urban cultural economy. The first trend is marketization. As seen in the case of homeowners in Shanghai happily occupied in home decoration, the variety of consumer choices are certainly liberating. They appreciate the material abundance of the contemporary era but also recognize that their newly gained freedom is ultimately limited by their ability to pay. Hierarchies and inequalities often take spatial forms, as in the haute-cuisine scene in Shanghai, where many upmarket international restaurants have opened in historical colonial buildings in the former concessions. The second trend is the influence of globalization on the urban cultural economy and the penetration of global consumer trends into local practices. This can be seen in almost all cases examined in the chapter, from Ms Zhang's changing wardrobe, to the arrival of international luxury brands, the presence of star chefs in Shanghai's upmarket restaurants, the new custom of sidewalk cafes at Xintiandi, and the integration of Chinese artists into the international art market. To examine the cultural economy in China, it is imperative to situate Chinese cities in the global network of cultural production. The last trend is the resurfacing of state control over cultural production. In nightlife and arts districts, new forms of state control can be clearly observed. The once seedy and ungovernable clubbing scenes in the 1990s were not favored by the government, which began several crackdown campaigns and eventually eliminated these organic nightlife spaces. Realizing the significance of a cosmopolitan nightlife for attracting tourism, business, and talent, since 2000, the local governments have actively supported private development of upmarket, high-end entertainment districts such as Xintiandi, where nightlife is safe, sanitized, and also closely watched by both public and private security forces. State control can be even more clearly observed in arts districts such as Songzhuang, where government officials are cross-appointed to the boards of management committees for supervising artists and of business enterprises for developing land. Art festivals frequently take place in Songzhuang, but what is allowed to be displayed often depends on the moral judgments of local officials and the departments of propaganda. The urban cultural economy – both the examples covered in this chapter and areas not examined here, such as publishing, broadcasting, film, and the music industry – has become a contentious field where new forms of government intervention have emerged so that the state can monitor and, at the same time, profit from the burgeoning cultural industries.

Conclusion

In an essay in *Public Culture* (forthcoming, 2013), urban theorist Neil Brenner points out that urbanization should not be understood simply as demographic trends, such as certain percentages of people living in cities, or as settlement types, such as Central Business Districts, gated communities, ghettos, suburbs, and exurbs. Rather, "the urban" should be understood as a process, one that is integral to the larger dynamics of global capitalism. The "urban process" entails certain "moments" and "effects" that should be positioned at the center of critical urban studies, such as the concentration and extension of the flows of people, goods, activities, infrastructure, and information, the creation and creative destruction of landscapes, and new forms of political consciousness and practices in everyday life (Brenner, 2013). The notion of "the urban" as a process is useful here to help unpack what Chinese urbanization means and entails.

Chinese urbanization has unmistakably involved major demographic shifts, as manifested in the changing ratio of the "urban" and "rural" populations. Chapter 1 discusses China's urban transition in this light. China always had a larger rural population than its urban population in the twentieth century. The urbanization level in 1980 was about 20 percent, and it increased to 26 percent by 1990, and to 36 percent in 2000. The first decade of the twenty-first century witnessed the most explosive urban population growth so far. Between 2000 and 2010, China's urban population expanded by over 200 million, and currently half of all Chinese people live in "urban areas."

The rapid urban population growth in the past decade has been driven primarily by migration and reclassification of cities. The 2010 census counted 221 million migrants, most of whom are from rural areas. Moreover, many "non-urban" areas have been reclassified as "urban," as rural counties are converted into cities and cities expand outward and annex the surrounding rural areas into their own districts.

More than the demographic shifts, Chinese urbanization also entails radical changes in the landscape and land use, and chapter 3 examines a variety of settlement types – both old and new – that are ubiquitously observed in Chinese cities today. At city centers, one can find business districts, historical preservation zones, demolition sites, new architectural icons, and residential *xiaoqu*, and, on the periphery, one can find massive satellite new towns, university towns, exclusive villas, artist villages, migrant enclaves, manufacturing zones, and the very new eco-cities. Chapter 3 discusses the messy process of making, remaking, and unmaking of urban landscapes. It shows how the variegated settlement types are products of Chinese state power and transnational flows, and how many of the new urban spaces have become sites for contestation, mobilization, and resistance. Urbanization inevitably involves the remaking of the landscape, but our understanding of the urban process should not be confined to changes in the land use only. We need to dig deeper to uncover the underlying dynamics that produce new urban spaces in China.

Beyond demographic shifts and landscape transformations, Chinese urbanization has also led to an overhaul of governing institutions and strategies, which are discussed in chapter 2. The old socialist institutions have been either dismantled or adapted to the new urban condition. At the neighborhood level, the "community" (*shequ*) was introduced in the 1990s amidst the retreat of the socialist welfare state and the collapse of the *danwei* system. Together with homeowners' associations, the "community" has become a key governing institution at the neighborhood level, organizing the propertied Chinese middle class to manage their neighborhood affairs, while at the same time enabling the state to continue exerting social control. At the scale of mega-city regions, such as the Pearl River Delta, competition, rather than coordination and collaboration, dominates inter-governmental relations, and there has yet to emerge a region-wide governing framework that can coordinate the development plans of different cities. Chapter 2 also discusses infrastructure-financing deals between local governments and state banks, and how urban infrastructure projects are often turned into profit-making machines by the private–public partnerships that own them. In the land sector, as revenues from land leasing have become the major source of local governments' income, municipal officials employ various tactics to evade orders from the center and continue to evict farmers and lease land to investors. In the housing sector, the market reform has turned China into a country with one of the highest homeownership rates in the world. Housing prices have kept rising, to the point that they are unaffordable for the majority of residents, but, as local governments have vested interests in the real-estate sector, the housing market is unlikely to cool down in the near future. Overall, chapter 2 shows that decision-making power has shifted from central ministries to territorial authorities, especially to city governments, which have substantial control over the development of land, housing, and infrastructure. Decentralization in China is largely a competitive process, as seen in the struggle by the central government to assert control through regulations and local strategies to resist such regulations in favor of promoting growth within localities.

Urbanization in China has given rise to new forms of inequality, and chapter 5 discusses types of both social and spatial inequality that have emerged in recent years, as well as the popular attitudes toward the increasing inequality. Market institutions have reduced older forms of social inequality that existed before 1978, and political connections are rewarded less as compared to human capital and entrepreneurial skills, but historical and institutional legacies of the socialist era persisted through the transition period and continue to determine the life chances of individuals. The most evident example of such legacies is *hukou* and its impact on income, education, and housing inequality. One interesting perspective in the recent studies on social stratification is the concept of categorical inequality (Wang, 2008), that is, the notion that there has been increasing inequality between groups and relative egalitarianism within groups, and a primary example of such group membership is the city – the life chances of individuals are largely structured by which city they live in. In terms of spatial inequality, geographers note three types of neighborhoods with concentrated poverty: old inner-city neighborhoods, degraded workers' villages, and the ViCs where migrant workers live. While the population under the Minimum Living Standard Program has been swelling, urbanization has brought great wealth to a few, such as real-estate tycoons and billionaire landlords. The survey results on the Chinese popular perception of inequality are quite striking. The most recent survey conducted by Martin Whyte and colleagues shows that the average Chinese citizen is largely approving and accepting of inequality, especially in the disadvantaged rural sector. Chapter 5 offers a few tentative explanations, but it is apparent that further surveys and studies are needed to examine whether this will continue to be the case, and why.

Finally, probably the most significant consequences of urbanization in China are the changes it has brought to the notions of citizenship and rights. These changes are most evident in the case of migrant workers, as discussed in chapter 4. Since the 1950s, China has always been a two-class society, divided into urban and rural citizens, and the latter have been exploited and forced to make various sacrifices for the country's modernization and industrialization projects. The *hukou* system has been relaxed to allow rural residents to look for work outside their villages and towns, but the basic premise of *hukou* remains unchanged – that is, to make the rural population second-class citizens in their own country, with fewer rights and entitlements. While living and working in cities, migrant workers are denied access to the welfare benefits accorded to their urban counterparts. The institutional discrimination by *hukou* status has deep implications in everyday life, and especially for the second generation of migrants who were born after 1980 and grew up in cities. They see themselves as urbanites but are reminded all the time that they are not the same as their peers who are urban *hukou* holders. Chapter 4 discusses the formation of ViCs to accommodate migrant workers who cannot find housing in the formal housing sector, and examines labor practices in mega-factories in the Special Economic Zone of Shenzhen, a city of 10 million residents among whom only 2 million have Shenzhen *hukou*. There has been a shift from rights-based to interest-based labor protests, as workers demand not only the rights guaranteed to them by law, such as the minimum wage, but also what they see as appropriate treatment for them as equal citizens – for example, higher wages and better benefits. Labor protests have become more violent and confrontational, and the pressure from the center to maintain stability has spurred local governments to engage protesters both through legal channels and on the streets. These various trends in migration, labor protests, and state responses signal the remaking of the two-class society brought about by urbanization, as migrant workers claim the right to the city they inhabit.

This book has tried to convey to readers the massive urban social change unfolding in China – the most populous country in the world. After more than 30 years of breakneck economic growth, Chinese cities have become very different places from their former socialist selves. Chinese urbanization entails new forms of governance, wealth, poverty, and, most importantly, new notions of citizenship. An urbanized China has deep implications, such as the emergence of the gigantic domestic market, a rising middle class, and a vibrant urban cultural scene, but the most significant change brought about by the urban process is the beginning of the end of the two-class structure of Chinese citizenship that has existed for six decades.

Notes

Chapter 1 China Urbanized

1 *China Statistical Yearbook*, 2011.

2 *Hukou* is the household registration system instituted in the 1950s that divides the national population into urban and rural sectors. See further discussions on *hukou* in chapter 2 with regard to governance, and chapter 4 in the context of migration.

3 China's One-Child policy was implemented in 1978 and it applies to urban couples. The rural population, ethnic minorities, and parents without siblings are allowed to have a second child. On the origins and evolution of the One-Child policy, see Greenhalgh (2008).

4 National Bureau of Statistics, at http://www.stats.gov.cn (accessed on June 1, 2011).

5 Central Intelligence Agency, *The World Factbook: Urbanization*, at https://www.cia.gov/library/publications/the-world-factbook/fields/2212.html (accessed on June 24, 2012).

6 Skinner's concept of "macro-regions" has been criticized for its lack of consideration of cross-regional connections as well as its rigid view of spaces as containers of social activities and relations. See Cartier (2002).

7 China's Five-Year Plans are policy documents issued once every five years, stating major economic development agendas for the whole country.

Chapter 2 Governance

1 "In Chongqing, hapless farmers yield to dozers," *Caixin Online*, November 9, 2011, http://english.caixin.cn/2011-11-09/100324228.html (accessed on November 21, 2011).

2 "Chinese authorities raze an artist's studio," January 13, 2011, *New York Times*, http://www.nytimes.com/2011/01/13/world/asia/13china.html (accessed on January 13, 2011).

3 *The Second National Economic Census of 2008*, National Bureau of Statistics, at http://www.stats.gov.cn/english/newsandcomingevents/t20091225_402610168.htm (accessed on July 9, 2012).

4 The data on the GDP of Chinese provinces are from the National Bureau of Statistics of China at http://www.stats.gov.cn, and the data on the GDP of other countries are from the World Development Indicators (WDI) of the World Bank, at http://databank.worldbank.org (accessed on February 25, 2011). Also see "Comparing Chinese provinces with countries," *The Economist*, February 25, 2011, at http://www.economist.com/content/all_parities_china (accessed on February 25, 2011).

5 "Accused Chinese party members face harsh discipline," *New York Times*, June 14, 2012, at http://www.nytimes.com/2012/06/15/world/asia/accused-chinese-party-members-face-harsh-discipline.html?pagewanted=all (accessed on June 27, 2012).

6 *China Fact File*, http://www.gov.cn/english/2007-10/29/content_30395.htm (accessed on June 10, 2011).

7 *The Second National Economic Census of 2008*, National Bureau of Statistics, at http://www.stats.gov.cn/english/newsandcomingevents/t20091225_402610168.htm, (accessed on July 9, 2012).

8 "China unveils new top 500 companies list," September 3, 2011, at http://www.china.org.cn/business/2011-09/03/content_23344983.htm (accessed on July 9, 2012).

9 http://www.sinopec.com (accessed on July 11, 2012).

10 *Regulation on Hukou Registration of the People's Republic of China*, 1958; *Regulation on Residents' Personal Identification Cards in the PRC*, 1985.

11 "Chinese police shoot protesters," BBC News, December 7, 2005, http://news.bbc.co.uk/2/hi/asia-pacific/4507130.stm (accessed on July 1, 2011).

12 "Residents vote in Chinese village at center of protest," *New York Times*, February 1, 2012, at http://www.nytimes.com/2012/02/02/world/asia/residents-vote-in-chinese-village-at-center-of-protest.html (accessed on July 1, 2011).

13 "Yijidu tudi weifa weigui an jinwanqi" ("More than 10,000 illegal land use cases in the first quarter of the year"), *Xinjing Bao* (*The Beijing News*), April 19, 2011, at http://epaper.bjnews.com.cn/html/2011-04/19/content_222328.htm (accessed on July 8, 2011).

14 "Shouci tudi wenze, 73 guanyuan shouchu" ("Land use investigations, 73 officials disciplined"), *Xinjing Bao* (*The Beijing News*), July 8, 2011, at http://epaper.bjnews.com.cn/html/2011-07/08/content_251394.htm?div=-1 (accessed on July 8, 2011).

15 Ministry of Housing and Urban-Rural Development, at http://www.mohurd. gov.cn/xwfb/200909/t20090924_195419.html (accessed on January 2, 2012).

16 "Guojia tongjiju: 70 dazhong chengshi 4 yuefen fangjia shangzhang 12.8%" ("National Bureau of Statistics: 70 large and medium city housing prices increased by 12.8% in April") May 11, 2010, at http://house.focus.cn/ news/2010-05-11/930238.html (accessed on July 10, 2012).

17 "Major property developer says offices ransacked by homeowners," *Caixin Online*, November 16, 2011, at http://english.caixin.cn/2011-11-16/ 100326936.html (accessed on January 2, 2012).

18 "Building boom in China stirs fears of debt overload," *New York Times*, July 7, 2011, at http://www.nytimes.com/2011/07/07/business/global/building-binge-by-chinas-cities-threatens-countrys-economic-boom. html?pagewanted=all (accessed on July 7, 2011).

19 "2010 nian tudi jiaoyi huobao, Beijing Shanghai maidi shouru poqianyi (Land transactions set new record in 2010, Beijing and Shanghai pocketed more than 100 billion)," at http://finance.jrj.com.cn/house/2010/11/ 2310128624532.shtml, November 23, 2010 (accessed on July 7, 2011).

20 "Building boom in China stirs fears of debt overload," *New York Times*, July 7, 2011, at http://www.nytimes.com/2011/07/07/business/global/ building-binge-by-chinas-cities-threatens-countrys-economic-boom. html?pagewanted=all (accessed on July 7, 2011).

21 Ibid.

22 "State Council delivers boost for logistics," *Global Times*, June 10, 2011, at http://business.globaltimes.cn/china-economy/2011-06/663729.html (accessed on June 10, 2011).

23 "Guojia wu buwei bushu shoufei gonglu zhuanxiang qingli (Five ministries order cleanup of highway charges)," July 11, 2011, at http://www.chinahighway.com/news/2011/551251.php (accessed on July 15, 2011).

24 "Guangshen gaosu rijun shoufei qianwan renminbi, beicheng quizhuanqian gonglu (Guangzhou-Shenzhen Expressway takes in 10 million every day, the most profitable road)," June 22, 2011, at http://news.qq.com/a/ 20110622/000390.htm (accessed on June 22, 2011).

25 "Trouble on the highway," *Caixin Online*, June 29, 2011, at http://english. caixin.cn/2011-06-29/100274315.html (accessed on October 1, 2011).

Chapter 3 Landscape

1 "Jianshebu diaocha CBD paome (The Ministry of Construction surveys the CBD bubble)," March 30, 2003, at http://business.sohu.com/26/33/ article207863326.shtml, (accessed on June 30, 2012).

2 Beijing Urban Planning Association.

3 "Liang Sicheng Lin Huiyin Guju: Yici yitu mohu de chaichu (The former residence of Liang Sicheng and Lin Huiyin: demolition without a clear cause)," *Lifeweek*, February 14, 2012, at http://www.lifeweek.com.cn/2012/0214/36422.shtml (accessed on June 30, 2012).

4 Interview with Ai Weiwei, August 12, 2006.

5 The controversy over the National Stadium also became a turning point for the career of Ai Weiwei – by now probably the best-known living Chinese artist in the world. Since the project, Ai Weiwei has grown increasingly critical of the government. His activism – including gathering the names of children who died during the Wenchuan earthquake in 2008 and organizing a street demonstration near Tian'anmen Square to protest demolitions of artist villages in 2010 – has greatly angered the authorities. In 2011, his newly completed Shanghai studio was demolished by government order and, soon after, he was arrested at the airport on his way to Hong Kong and then detained for several months. Ai Weiwei was finally released in August 2011 but was fined over 1 million RMB on charges of tax evasion.

6 See chapter 4 on migrant villages, or ViCs.

7 See Hassenpflug (2010) for a detailed discussion of the urban design and planning of Anting and Songjiang new towns.

8 See the documentary film *Manufactured Landscapes* (2006), directed by Jennifer Baichwal, which follows photographer Edward Burtynsky as he travels in China and observes changes in the landscape due to industrial manufacturing.

9 "China's cancer villages reveal dark side of economic boom," the *Guardian*, June 7, 2010, at http://www.guardian.co.uk/environment/2010/jun/07/china-cancer-villages-industrial-pollution (accessed on December 16, 2011).

10 "New Five-Year Plan called 'revolutionary'," *Asia Times Online*, October 13, 2005, at http://www.atimes.com/atimes/China_Business/GJ13Cb01.html (accessed on December 16, 2011).

11 Computed by the author from the Ministry of Environmental Protection's list of National Model Cities for Environmental Protection as of 2012. The list is available in Chinese at http://wfs.mep.gov.cn/pv_obj_cache/pv_obj_id_F025E2CE1E377E3A8143300351132796DBFA0000/filename/P020120116499615667950.pdf (accessed on March 10, 2012).

12 "China's city of the future rises on a wasteland," *New York Times*, September 28, 2011, at http://www.nytimes.com/cwire/2011/09/28/28climatewire-chinas-city-of-the-future-rises-on-a-wastela-76934.html?pagewanted=all (accessed on December 16, 2011).

13 "China aims for 'ecological civilization,'" *China Daily*, July 17, 2011, at http://www.chinadaily.com.cn/china/2011-07/17/content_12919396.htm; "China plans to have 100 new energy demonstration cities by 2015," *Business China*, April 27, 2011, at http://en.21cbh.com/HTML/2011-4-27/zMMjMyXz-IxMDAzMw.html (accessed on December 16, 2011).

14 "Shenzhen's achievements in solar industry," *Renewable Energy World*, April 27, 2011, at http://www.renewableenergyworld.com/rea/partner/asia-solar-expo/news/article/2011/04/shenzhens-achievements-in-solar-industry (accessed on December 16, 2011).

15 See: http://www.tianjinecocity.gov.sg/Features.htm (accessed on February 8, 2012).

16 "Building China's 21st century megacity: Shanghai's experiment with water and nature," September 30, 2011, at http://www.circleofblue.org/waternews/2011/world/manmade-lake-and-nature-preserve-at-center-of-new-shanghai-borough/ (accessed on December 16, 2011).

Chapter 4 Migration

1 "2010 nian chunyun zhengshi kaishi, yuji keliuliang jiang chaoguo 25 yi renci (2010 spring traffic starts, 2.5 billion travels estimated)," at http://cd.qq.com/a/20100130/000967.htm (accessed on October 2, 2011).

2 REAP (Rural Education Action Project), Stanford University, at http://reap.stanford.edu/docs/about_REAP/ (accessed on October 2, 2011).

3 See a detailed discussion in Chung (2000) on the difference between *chengzhongcun*, or Villages-in-the-City, and urban villages in the West.

4 Shenzhen City Government, at http://english.sz.gov.cn/gi/ (accessed on July 11, 2012).

5 *Temporary Regulations on ViCs in Shenzhen (2004), Suggestions for Implementations of the Temporary Regulations on ViCs in Shenzhen (2005), Comprehensive Plan for Redeveloping ViCs in Shenzhen, 2005–2010 (2005); and Shenzhen Urban Renewal Specific Plan, 2010–2015 (2010).*

6 *Shenzhen News*, December 21, 2011, at http://news.sznews.com/content/2011-12/21/content_6326669.htm (accessed on December 22, 2011).

7 "Air-raid warnings: as the leaders see it, a plague of human rats in the capital," *The Economist*, February 17, 2011, at http://www.economist.com/node/18184564/comments?page=1 (accessed on February 30, 2011).

8 "China's bosses are abandoning ship," *Los Angeles Times*, November 3, 2008, at http://articles.latimes.com/2008/nov/03/business/fi-factory3 (accessed on October 21, 2011).

9 http://www.ico-china.org (accessed on February 6, 2011).

Chapter 5 Inequality

1 Ministry of Housing and Urban-Rural Development, http://www.mohurd. gov.cn/xwfb/200909/t20090924_195419.html (accessed on January 2, 2012).

2 "Guo Meimei Deep sorry," at http://www.china.org.cn/china/2011-08/04/ content_23139500.htm, August 4, 2011, and "Guo Meimei Red Cross controversy pissing off Chinese netizens", June 29, 2011, at www.chinasmack.com (accessed on July 12, 2012).

Chapter 6 Cultural Economy

1 In 2011, Da Vinci, an Italian-Chinese joint-venture company specializing in high-end furniture, was taken to court for mislabeling furniture made in factories in Guangdong as "Made in Italy," and charging exorbitant prices. See *The Beijing News*, July 11, 2011, at http://epaper.bjnews.com.cn/html/2011-07/11/content_252301.htm?div=-1 (accessed on July 15, 2011).

2 Interview with Cui Dabai, the head of Xiaopu Village by Meng Sun, July 15, 2009.

Bibliography

Abramson, Daniel. 2007. "The dialectics of urban planning in China," in Fulong Wu, ed., *China's Emerging Cities: The Making of New Urbanism*. New York: Routledge, 66–86.

Anagnost, Ann. 2008. "From 'class' to 'social strata': Grasping the social totality in reform-era China." *Third World Quarterly* 29(3): 497–519.

Angremy, Berenice. 2008. "798, a place of artistic possibilities," in Rui Huang, ed., *Beijing 798*. Chengdu: Sichuan Fine Arts Publishing House, 12–21.

Appleton, Simon, and Lina Song. 2007. "The myth of the 'new urban poverty'? Trends in urban poverty in China, 1988–2002," in John Logan, ed., *Urban China in Transition*. Oxford: Blackwell, 64–85.

Arrighi, Giovanni. 2007. *Adam Smith in Beijing: Lineages of the Twenty-First Century*. London and New York: Verso.

Beijing Municipal Planning Commission. 2004. *The National Stadium*. Beijing: China Architecture and Building Press.

Béja, Jean-Philippe. 2006. "The changing aspects of civil society in China." *Social Research* 73(1): 53–74.

Bian, Yanjie, and John Logan. 1996. "Market transition and the persistence of power: The changing stratification system in China." *American Sociological Review* 61(5): 739–58.

Boland, Alana, and Jiangang Zhu. 2012. "Public participation in China's green communities: Mobilizing memories and structuring incentives." *Geoforum* 43(1): 147–57.

Bray, David. 2005. *Social Space and Governance in Urban China: The Danwei System from Origins to Urban Reform*. Stanford, CA: Stanford University Press.

Bray, David. 2006. "Building 'community': New strategies of governance in urban China." *Economy and Society* 35(4): 530–49.

Bray, David. 2008. "Designing to govern: Space and power in two Wuhan communities." *Built Environment* 34(4): 392–407.

Brenner, Neil. "Theses on urbanization." *Public Culture*, 25, 1, (2013): 85-114.

Brenner, Neil, and Nik Theodore. 2002. *Space of Neoliberalism: Urban Restructuring in North America and West Europe*. New York: Oxford University Press.

Brenner, Neil, Peter Marcuse, and Margit Mayer, eds. 2011. *Cities for People, Not for Profit: Critical Urban Theory and the Right to the City*. New York: Routledge.

Cai, Yongshun. 2005. "China's moderate middle class: The case of homeowners' resistance." *Asian Survey* 45(5): 777–99.

Campanella, Thomas. 2008. *The Concrete Dragon: China's Urban Revolution and What It Means for the World*. Princeton, NJ: Princeton Architecture Press.

Cartier, Carolyn. 2002. "Origins and evolution of a geographical idea: The 'macroregion' in China." *Modern China* 28(1): 79–143.

Chan, Anita. 2011. "Strikes in China's export industries in comparative perspective." *The China Journal* 65: 27–51.

Chan, Kam Wing. 1996. "Post-Mao China: A two class urban society in the making." *International Journal of Urban and Regional Research* 20(1): 134–50.

Chan, Kam Wing. 2009. "The Chinese *hukou* system at 50." *Eurasian Geography and Economics* 50(2): 197–221.

Chan, Kam Wing, and Will Buckingham. 2008. "Is China abolishing the *hukou* system?" *The China Quarterly*: 195: 582–606.

Chang, Sen-dou. 1977. "The morphology of walled capitals," in G. William Skinner, ed., *The City in Late Imperial China*. Stanford, CA: Stanford University Press, 75–100.

Chen, Guo, Chaolin Gu, and Fulong Wu. 2006. "Urban poverty in the transitional economy: A case of Nanjing, China." *Habitat International* 30(1): 1–26.

Chen, Wending (ed.). 2011. *Weilai Meiyou Chengzhongcun (No Villages-in-the-City in the Future)*. Beijing: Zhongguo Minzhu Fazhi Press.

Chen, Xiangming. 1991. "China's city hierarchy, urban policy and spatial development in the 1980s." *Urban Studies* 28(3): 341–67.

Chew, Matthew. 2010. "Research on Chinese nightlife cultures and night-time economies." *Chinese Sociology and Anthropology* 42(2): 3–21.

Chung, Him. 2010. "Building an image of villages-in-the-city: A clarification of China's distinct urban spaces." *International Journal of Urban and Regional Research* 34(2): 421–37.

Cohen, Philip N., and Feng Wang. 2008. "Market and gender pay equity: Have Chinese reforms narrowed the gap?" in Deborah Davis and Feng Wang, eds, *Creative Wealth and Poverty in Postsocialist China*. Stanford, CA: Stanford University Press, 37–53.

Davis, Deborah. 2005. "Urban consumer culture." *The China Quarterly* 183: 692–709.

Davis, Deborah, and Feng Wang, eds. 2009. *Creating Wealth and Poverty in Postsocialist China*. Stanford, CA: Stanford University Press.

Denton, Kirk. 2005. "Museums, memorial sites and exhibitionary culture in the People's Republic of China." *The China Quarterly* 183: 565–86.

Dong, Madeleine Yue. 2003. *Republican Beijing: The City and Its Histories*. Berkeley, CA: University of California Press.

Elvin, Mark. 1974. "The administration of Shanghai: 1905–1914," in Mark Elvin and G. William Skinner, eds, *The Chinese City between Two Worlds*. Stanford, CA: Stanford University Press, 239–62.

Fan, Cindy. 2008. *China on the Move*. New York: Routledge.

Farrer, James. 2010a. "Eating the West and beating the rest: Culinary Occidentalism and urban soft power in Asia's global food cities," in James Farrer, ed., *Globalization, Food and Social Identities in the Asia Pacific Region*. Tokyo: Sophia University Institute of Comparative Culture, 1–21. At http://icc.fla. sophia.ac.jp/global%20food%20papers/pdf/2_3_FARRER.pdf

Farrer, James. 2010b. "Shanghai bars: Patchwork globalization and flexible cosmopolitanism in reform-era urban-leisure spaces." *Chinese Sociology and Anthropology* 42(2): 22–38.

Farrer, James. 2011. "Global nightscapes in Shanghai as ethnosexual contact zones." *The Journal of Ethnic and Migration Studies* 37(5): 747–64.

Farrer, James, and Andrew Field. Forthcoming, 2013. "From interzone to transzone: Race and sex in the contact zones of Shanghai's global nightlife." *Intersections: Gender and Sexuality in Asia and the Pacific* 33.

Fei, Xiaotong. 1986. *Small Towns in China: Functions, Problems, and Prospects*. Beijing: New World Press.

Feng, Jian, and Yixing Zhou. 2003. "1990 niandai Beijing shi renkou kongjian fenbu de zuixin bianhua (The latest development in demographic spatial distribution in Beijing in the 1990s)." *Chengshi Guihua* 27: 55–63.

Feuerwerker, Albert. 1983. "The foreign presence in China," in John K. Fairbank, ed., *Republican China 1912–1949*, Part 1. Cambridge Histories Online, Cambridge University Press, at DOI:10.1017/CHOL9780521235419.004 (accessed on April 3, 2012).

Field, Andrew. 2010. *Shanghai's Dancing World: Cabaret Culture and Urban Politics, 1919–1954*. Hong Kong: Chinese University Press.

Friedman, Eli, and Ching Kwan Lee. 2010. "Remaking the world of Chinese labour: A 30-year retrospective." *British Journal of Industrial Relations* 48(3): 507–33.

Friedmann, John. 2005. *China's Urban Transition*. Minneapolis, MN: University of Minnesota Press.

Froissart, Chole. 2006. "Escaping from under the Party's thumb: A few examples of migrant workers' strivings for autonomy." *Social Research* 73(1): 197–218.

Gallagher, Mary. 2004. "The limits of civil society in a late Leninist state," in Muthiah Alagappa, ed., *Civil Society and Political Change in Asia: Expanding and Contracting Democratic Space*. Stanford, CA: Stanford University Press, 419–52.

Gallagher, Mary. 2007. "Hope for protection and hopeless choices: Labor legal aid in the PRC," in Elizabeth Perry and Merle Goldman, eds, *Grassroots Political Reform in Contemporary China*. Cambridge, MA: Harvard University Press, 196–227.

Gaubatz, Piper. 2005. "Globalization and the development of new Central Business Districts in Beijing, Shanghai, and Guangzhou," in Fulong Wu and Laurence Ma, eds, *Restructuring the Chinese City*. New York and Oxford: Routledge, 98–121.

Giroir, Guillaume. 2006. "A globalized golden ghetto in a Chinese garden: The Fontainebleau villas in Shanghai," in Fulong Wu, ed., *Globalization and the Chinese City*. New York: Routledge, 208–25.

Goodman, David. 2008. "Why China has no new middle class: Cadres, managers, and entrepreneurs," in David Goodman, ed., *The New Rich in China: Future Rulers, Present Lives*. New York: Routledge, 23–37.

Greenhalgh, Susan. 2008. *Just One Child: Science and Policy in Deng's China*. Berkeley, CA: University of California Press.

Guthrie, Doug. 2008. *China and Globalization*. New York: Routledge.

Harvey, David. 1989. "From managerialism to entrepreneurialism: The transformation of governance in late capitalism." *Geografiska Annaler* 71B: 3–17.

Harvey, David. 2005. *A Brief History of Neoliberalism*. New York: Oxford University Press.

Hassenpflug, Dieter. 2010. *The Urban Code of China*. Basel: Birkhauser GmbH.

He, Shenjing, and Fulong Wu. 2009. "China's emerging neoliberal urbanism: Perspectives from urban redevelopment." *Antipode* 41(2): 282–304.

He, Shenjing, Fulong Wu, Chris Webster, and Yuting Liu. 2010. "Poverty concentration and determinants in China's urban low-income neighbourhoods and social groups." *International Journal of Urban and Regional Research* 34(2): 328–49.

Hsing, You Tien. 2006. "Land and territorial politics in urban China." *The China Quarterly* 187: 575–91.

Hsing, You Tien. 2010. *The Great Urban Transformation: Politics of Land and Property in China*. New York: Oxford University Press.

Hsu, Jennifer Yuan-Jean. 2007. "Defining boundaries of the relationship: Beijing migrant civil society organizations and the government." *Graduate Journal of Asia-Pacific Studies* 5: 16–33.

Huang, Rui. 2008. "1, 2, 3, 4, 5, 6, 798," in Rui Huang, ed., *Beijing 798*. Chengdu: Sichuan Fine Arts Publishing House, 2–10.

Huang, Yasheng. 2008. *Capitalism with Chinese Characteristics: Entrepreneurship and the State.* New York: Cambridge University Press.

Huang, Youqin. 2003. "A room of one's own: Housing consumption and residential crowding in transitional urban China." *Environment and Planning A* 35(4): 591–614.

Huang, Youqin. 2006. "Collectivism, political control, and gating in Chinese cities." *Urban Geography* 27(6): 507–25.

Huang, Youqin, and Leiwen Jiang. 2009. "Housing inequality in transitional Beijing." *International Journal of Urban and Regional Research* 33(4): 936–56.

Johnson, Ian. 2004. *Wild Grass: Three Stories of Change in Modern China.* New York: Pantheon Books.

Keane, Michael. 2006. "From made in China to created in China." *International Journal of Cultural Studies* 9(3): 285–96.

Keane, Michael. 2007. *Created in China: The Great New Leap Forward.* London: Routledge Curzon.

Kharas, Homi. 2010. "The emerging middle class in developing countries." OECD Development Centre, Working paper no.285, at http://www.oecd.org/dev/wp (accessed on July 15, 2012).

Kirkby, Richard. 1985. *Urbanization in China: Town and Country in a Developing Economy.* New York: Columbia University Press.

Kwong, Julia. 2004. Educating migrant children: Negotiations between the state and civil society. *The China Quarterly* 180: 1073–88.

Leaf, Michael, and Li Hou. 2006. "The 'third-spring' of urban planning in China." *China Information* 20(3): 553–38.

Lee, Ching Kwan. 2007. *Against the Law: Labor Protests in China's Rustbelt and Sunbelt.* Berkeley and Los Angeles, CA: University of California Press.

Lee, Ching Kwan, and Yuan Shen. 2009. "China: The paradox and possibility of a public sociology of labor." *Work and Occupations* 36(2): 110–25.

Leung, C. K. 1996. "Foreign manufacturing investment and regional industrial growth in Guangdong province, China." *Environment and Planning A* 28(3): 513–36.

Li, Si-ming, Yuhua Zhu, and Limei Li. 2012. "Neighborhood type, gatedness, and residential experiences in Chinese cities: A study of Guangzhou." *Urban Geography* 33(2): 237–55.

Li, Yun, and Zilai Tang. 2005. "1982–2000 nian shanghai shi jiaoqu shehui kongjian jiegou jiqi yanhua (Transformation of social space structure in the suburban areas of Shanghai from 1980 to 2000)." *Urban Planning Forum* 160: 27–36.

Li, Yuwai, Bo Miao, and Graeme Lang. 2011. "The local environmental state in China." *The China Quarterly* 205: 115–32.

Liang, Zai, Lin Guo and Charles Chengrong Duan. 2008. "Migration and the well-being of children in China." *Yale China Health Journal* 5: 25–46.

Lieberthal, Kenneth. 2004. *Governing China: From Revolution through Reform.* New York: Norton.

Lin, George. 2002. "The growth and structural change of Chinese cities: A contextual and geographic analysis." *Cities* 19(5): 299–316.

Lin, George. 2007. "Chinese urbanism in question: State, society, and the reproduction of urban spaces." *Urban Geography* 28(1): 7–29.

Lin, George. 2009. *Developing China: Land, Politics and Social Conditions.* London: Routledge.

Lin, George, and Samuel P. S. Ho. 2005. "The state, land system, and land development processes in contemporary China." *Annals of the Association of American Geographer* 95(2): 411–36.

Lin, Nan. 1995. "Local market socialism: Local corporatism in action in rural China." *Theory and Society* 24(3): 301–54.

Lin, Yi. 2011. "Turning rurality into modernity: Suzhi education in a suburban public school of migrant children in Xiamen." *The China Quarterly* 206: 313–30.

Liu, Haiyan, and Kristin Stapleton. 2006. "Chinese urban history: States of the field." *China Information* 20(3): 391–427.

Liu, Yuting, and Fulong Wu. 2006. "Urban poverty neighbourhoods: Typology and spatial concentration under China's market transition, a case study of Nanjing." *Geoforum* 37(4): 610–26.

Logan, John, Yanjie Bian, and F. Bian. 1999. "Housing inequality in urban China in the 1990s." *International Journal of Urban and Regional Research* 23(1): 7–25.

Lu, Hanchao. 1999. *Beyond the Neon Lights: Everyday Shanghai in the Early Twentieth Century.* Berkeley, CA: University of California Press.

Ma, Laurence. 2005. "Urban administrative restructuring, changing scale relations and local economic development in China." *Political Geography* 24(4): 477–97.

Ma, Laurence. 2006. "The state of the field of urban China: A critical multidisciplinary overview of the literature." *China Information* 20(3): 363–89.

Ma, Laurence, and Gonghao Cui. 2002. "Economic transition at the local level: Diverse forms of town development in China." *Eurasian Geography and Economics* 43(2): 79–103.

May, Shannon. 2008. "Ecological citizenship and a plan for sustainable development: Lessons from Huangbaiyu." *City* 12(2): 237–44.

Mayer, Margit. 2009. "The 'right to the city' in the context of shifting mottos of urban social movements." *City* 13(2–3): 362–74.

Miao, Pu. 2003. "Deserted streets in a jammed town: The gated community in Chinese cities and its solution." *Journal of Urban Design* 8(1): 45–66.

Mote, F. W. 1977. "The transformation of Nanking, 1350–1400," in G. William Skinner, ed., *The City in Late Imperial China*. Stanford, CA: Stanford University Press, 101–54.

Murphy, Rachel. 2002. *How Migrant Labor is Changing Rural China*. Cambridge: Cambridge University Press.

Murphy, Rhoads. 1974. "The treaty ports and China's modernization," in Mark Elvin and William Skinner, eds, *The Chinese City between Two Worlds*. Stanford, CA: Stanford University Press, 17–71.

Naquin, Susan. 2000. *Temples and City Life, 1400–1900*. Berkeley, CA: University of California Press.

Naughton, Barry. 1995. "Cities in the Chinese economic system: Changing roles and conditions for autonomy," in Deborah Davis, ed., *Urban Spaces in Contemporary China: The Potential for Autonomy and Community in Post-Mao China*. New York: Cambridge University Press, 61–89.

Nee, Victor. 1989. "A theory of market transition: From redistribution to markets in state socialism." *American Sociological Review* 54(5): 663–81.

Ngai, Pun, and Jenny Chan. 2012. "Global capital, the state, and Chinese workers: The Foxconn experience." *Modern China* 38(4): 383–410.

Nye, Joseph. 2005. "The rise of China's soft power." *Wall Street Journal Asia*. At http://belfercenter.ksg.harvard.edu/publication/1499/rise_of_chinas_soft_power.html (accessed on July 15, 2012).

O'Brien, Kevin J., and Lianjiang Li. 2006. *Rightful Resistance in Rural China*. New York: Cambridge University Press.

Oi, Jean. 1992. "Fiscal reform and the economic foundations of local state corporatism in China." *World Politics* 45(1): 99–126.

Oi, Jean. 1999. *Rural China Takes Off*. Berkeley, CA: University of California Press.

Oi, Jean. 2010. "Political crosscurrents in China's corporate restructuring," in Jean Oi, Scott Rozelle, and Xueguang Zhou, eds., *Growing Pains: Tensions and*

Opportunity in China's Transformation. Stanford, CA: APARC Shorenstein, 5–26.

Olds, Kris. 1997. "Globalizing Shanghai: The 'global intelligence corps' and the building of Pudong." *Cities* 14(2): 109–23.

Pannell, Clifton. 2002. "China's continuing urban transition." *Environment and Planning A*, 34(9): 1571–89.

Pow, Choon-piew. 2009. *Gated Communities in China: Class, Privilege and the Moral Politics of the Good Life*. Abingdon, Oxon: Routledge.

Qi, Ye, Li Ma, Huanbo Zhang, and Huimin Li. 2008. "Translating a global issue into local priority: China's local government response to climate change." *The Journal of Environment and Development* 17(4): 379–400.

Read, Benjamin. 2003. "Democratizing the neighborhood? New private housing and home-owner self-organization in urban China." *The China Journal* 49: 31–59.

Ren, Xuefei. 2008a. "Architecture and China's urban revolution." *City* 12(2): 217–25.

Ren, Xuefei. 2008b. "Forward to the past: Historical preservation in globalizing Shanghai." *City and Community* 7(1): 23–43.

Ren, Xuefei. 2008c. "Architecture and nation building in the age of globalization." *Journal of Urban Affairs* 30(2): 175–90.

Ren, Xuefei. 2009. "Olympic Beijing: Reflections on urban space and global connectivity." *International Journal of the History of Sports* 26(8): 1011–39.

Ren, Xuefei. 2011. *Building Globalization: Transnational Architecture Production in Urban China*. Chicago, IL: University of Chicago Press.

Ren, Xuefei. 2012. "'Green' as spectacle in China," *Journal of International Affairs* 65(2): 19–30.

Ren, Xuefei, and Meng Sun. 2012. "Artistic urbanization: Creative industries and creative control in Beijing." *International Journal of Urban and Regional Research* 36(3): 504–21.

Robinson, Jennifer. 2006. *Ordinary Cities*. London: Routledge.

Rowe, William. 1992. *Hankow: Commerce and Society in a Chinese City, 1796–1889*. Stanford, CA: Stanford University Press.

Saunier, Pierre-Yves. 2008. "Global city, take 2: A view from urban history," in Pierre-Yves Saunier and Shane Ewen, eds, *Another Global City: Historical Explorations into the Transnational Municipal Moment, 1850–2000*. New York: Palgrave Macmillan, 1–18.

Shambaugh, David. 2008. *China's Communist Party: Atrophy and Adaptation*. Washington, DC: Woodrow Wilson Center Press.

Shen, Jianfa. 2007. "Scale, state and the city: Urban transformation in post–reform China." *Habitat International* 31(3–4): 303–16.

Shi, Weidong, Qufu He, and Jinchao Fan. 2010. *Zhongguo Tongxian Zhengqu he Xianxia Zhengqu de Lishi Fazhan yu Dangdai Gaige (The Historical Development and Contemporary Reform of China's County System)*. Nanjing: Southeast University Press.

Skinner, G. William. 1977. *The City in Late Imperial China*. Stanford, CA: Stanford University Press.

Smith, Chris, and Ngai Pun. 2006. "The dormitory labor regime in China as a site for control and resistance." *International Journal of Human Resource Management* 17(8): 1456–70.

Solinger, Dorothy J. 1999. *Contesting Citizenship in Urban China: Peasant Migrants, the State, and the Logic of the Market*. Berkeley and Los Angeles, CA: University of California Press.

Solinger, Dorothy J. 2006. "The creation of a new underclass in China and its implications." *Environment and Urbanization* 18(1): 177–93.

State Council. 1998. *Notice on Further Deepening Urban Housing Reform and Accelerating Housing Construction*. Beijing.

State Council. 2001. *The Tenth Five-Year Plan*, at http://www.china.com.cn/ch-15/plan8.htm (accessed on July 15, 2012).

State Council. 2003. *Notice on Promoting Continuous and Healthy Growth of the Real Estate Sector*. Beijing. At http://www.gov.cn/zwgk/2005-08/13/content_22259.htm (accessed on September 28, 2012).

Su, Yang, and Xin He. 2010. "Street as courtroom: State accommodation of labor protest in south China." *Law and Society Review* 44(1): 157–84.

Sudjic, Deyan. 1992. *The 100 Mile City*. San Diego, CA: Harcourt Brace.

Tan, Laura. 2006. "Revolutionary spaces in globalization: Beijing's Dashanzi Arts District." At http://www.yorku.ca/topia/docs/conference/Tan.pdf; accessed on July 15, 2012.

Tang, Wenfang, and Qing Yang. 2008. "The Chinese urban caste system in transition." *The China Quarterly* 196: 759–79.

Tomba, Luigi. 2005. "Residential space and collective interest formation in Beijing's housing disputes." *The China Quarterly* 184: 934–51.

Walder, Andrew. 1992. "Property rights and stratification in socialist redistributive economies." *American Sociological Review* 57(4): 524–39.

Walder, Andrew. 2010. "Irresolvable contradictions or growing pains? Perspectives on China's challenges," in Jean Oi, Scott Rozelle, and Xueguang Zhou, eds, *Growing Pains: Tensions and Opportunity in China's Transformation*. Stanford, CA: APARC Shorenstein, xiii–xxv.

Wang, Fei-ling. 2004. "Reformed migration control and new targeted people: China's *hukou* system in the 2000s." *The China Quarterly* 177: 115–32.

Wang, Feng. 2008. *Boundaries and Categories: Rising Inequality in Post-Socialist Urban China*. Stanford, CA: Stanford University Press.

Wang, Hui, Ran Tao, Lanlan Wang, and Fubing Su. 2010. "Farmland preservation and land development rights trading in Zhejiang, China." *Habitat International* 34(4): 454–63.

Wang, Jing. 2004. "The global reach of a new discourse: How far can 'cultural industries' travel?" *International Journal of Cultural Studies* 7(1): 9–19.

Wang, Jun. 2003. *Cheng Ji*. Beijing: Sanlian Press.

Wang, Jun. 2009. "'Art in capital': Shaping distinctiveness in a culture-led urban regeneration project in Red Town, Shanghai." *Cities* 26(6): 318–30.

Wang, Xiaobing, Chengfang Liu, Linxiu Zhang, Renfu Luo, Thomas Glauben, Yaojiang Shi, Scott Rozelle, and Brian Sharbono. 2011. "College education and the poor in China: Documenting the hurdles to educational attainment and college matriculation." *Asia Pacific Education Review* 12(4): 533–46.

Wang, Xiaobing, Chengfang Liu, Linxiu Zhang, Renfu Luo, and Scott Rozelle. 2011. "College is a rich, Han, urban, male club: Research notes from a census survey of four tier one colleges in China." At http://reap.stanford.edu/publications/list/0/0/2/; accessed on December 1, 2011.

Wang, Yaping, and Alan Murie. 1996. "The process of commercialization of urban housing in China." *Urban Studies*, 33(6): 971–89.

Wang, Yaping, and Alan Murie. 2000. "Social and spatial implications of housing reform in China." *International Journal of Urban and Regional Research*, 24(2): 397–417.

Wang, Yaping, Yangling Wang, and Jiansheng Wu. 2009. "Urbanization and informal development in China: Urban villages in Shenzhen." *International Journal of Urban and Regional Research* 33(4): 957–73.

Wasserstrom, Jeffrey. 2009. "Middle-class mobilization." *Journal of Democracy* 20(3): 29–32.

Weber, Max. 1958. *The City*. Glencoe, IL: Free Press.

Whyte, Martin. 2011. "Myth of the social volcano: Popular responses to rising inequality in China," in William Kirby, ed., *The People's Republic of China at 60: An International Assessment*. Cambridge, MA: Harvard University Asia Center, 273–90.

Whyte, Martin, and William Parish. 1984. *Urban Life in Contemporary China*. Chicago, IL: University of Chicago Press.

While, Aidan, Andrew Jonas, and David Gibbs. 2004. "The environment and the entrepreneurial city." *International Journal of Urban and Regional Research* 28(3): 549–69.

Wong, Edward. 2011. "Chinese authorities raze an artist's studio," January 13, 2011, *New York Times*, at http://www.nytimes.com/2011/01/13/world/asia/13china.html (accessed on January 13, 2011).

Wu, Chenguang. 2004. "Beijing aoyun shoushen diaocha." in *Nanfang Daily*, at http://www.politicalchina.org/NewsInfo.asp?NewsID=55035 (accessed on September 28, 2012).

Wu, Fulong. 2002. "China's changing urban governance in transition towards a more market-oriented economy." *Urban Studies* 39(7): 1071–93.

Wu, Fulong. 2007. "Re-orientation of the city plan: Strategic planning and design competition in China." *Geoforum* 38(2): 379–92.

Wu, Fulong. 2010a. "Gated and packaged suburbia: Packaging and branding Chinese suburban residential development." *Cities* 27(5): 385–96.

Wu, Fulong. 2010b. "Property rights, citizenship and the making of the new poor in urban China," in Fulong Wu and Chris Webster, eds, *Marginalization in Urban China: Comparative Perspectives*. Basingstoke, UK: Palgrave Macmillan, 72–89.

Wu, Fulong, and Fangzhu Zhang. 2010. "China's emerging city region governance: Toward a research framework." *Progress in Planning* 73: 60–3.

Wu, Fulong, Shenjing He, and Chris Webster. 2010. "Path dependency and the neighbourhood effect: Urban poverty in impoverished neighbourhoods in Chinese cities." *Environment and Planning A* 42(1): 134–52.

Wu, Hung. 2008. "Tui-Transfiguration." in *Beijing 798*. Chengdu: Sichuan Fine Arts Publishing House, 48–57.

Wu, Weiping. 2004. "Sources of migrant housing disadvantage in urban China." *Environment and Planning A* 36(7): 1285–1304.

Wu, Weiping. 2010a. "Urban infrastructure financing and economic performance in China." *Urban Geography* 31(5): 648–67.

Wu, Weiping. 2010b. "Drifting and getting stuck: Migrants in Chinese cities." *Cities* 14(1): 13–24.

Xu, Jiang, and Anthony Yeh. 2009. "Decoding urban land governance: State reconstruction in contemporary Chinese cities." *Urban Studies* 46(3): 559–81.

Xu, Jiang, and Anthony Yeh. 2010. "Planning mega city regions in China: Rationales and policies." *Progress in Planning* 73: 17–22.

Xu, Jiang, Anthony Yeh, and Fulong Wu. 2009. "Land commodification: New land development and politics in China since the late 1990s." *International Journal of Urban and Regional Research* 33(4): 890–913.

Xu, Zelai, and Nong Zhu. 2011. "City size distribution in China: Are large cities dominant?" *Urban Studies* 46(10): 2159–85.

Yang, Chun. 2006. "The geopolitics of cross-boundary governance in the Greater Pearl River Delta, China: A case study of the proposed Hong Kong-Zhuhai-Macau Bridge." *Political Geography* 25(7): 817–35.

Yang, Daniel You-Ren, and Hung-Kai Wang. 2008. "Dilemmas of local governance under the development zone fever in China: A case study of the Suzhou region." *Urban Studies* 45(5–6): 1037–54.

Ye, Ying. 2008. "Weightlessness – 798 in the present continuous tense." In Rui Huang, ed., *Beijing 798*. Chengdu: Sichuan Fine Arts Publishing House, 26–37.

Yeh, Anthony, and Fulong Wu. 1996. "The new land development process and urban development in Chinese cities." *International Journal of Urban and Regional Research* 20(2): 330–53.

Yip, Ngai-ming. 2012. "Walled without gates: Gated communities in Shanghai." *Urban Geography* 33(2): 221–36.

Zeng, Guohua. 2010. "The transformation of nightlife districts in Guangzhou, 1995–2009." *Chinese Sociology and Anthropology* 42(2): 56–75.

Zhang, Gan. 2011. "Theory and practice: The modern Chinese art museums." Paper presented at the conference *Contested Ground: Visual Culture in China after 1989*. University of Kentucky.

Zhang, Li. 2002. *Strangers in the City: Reconfigurations of Space, Power, and Social Networks within China's Floating Population*. Stanford, CA: Stanford University Press.

Zhang, Li. 2005. "Migrant enclaves and impacts of redevelopment policy in Chinese cities," in Laurence Ma and Fulong Wu, eds, *Restructuring the Chinese City: Changing Society, Economy and Space*. London: Routledge, 243–59.

Zhang, Li. 2010. *In Search of Paradise: Middle Class Living in a Chinese Metropolis*. Ithaca, NY: Cornell University Press.

Zhao, L. 2007. *The 2006–2007 China Art Market Research Report*. Wuhan: Hunan Art Publisher.

Zheng, Jane. 2010. "The entrepreneurial state in creative industry cluster development in Shanghai." *Journal of Urban Affairs* 32(2): 143–70.

Zhou, Yixing, and Laurence Ma. 2000. "Economic restructuring and suburbanization in China." *Urban Geography* 21(3): 205–36.

Zhou, Yixing, and Laurence Ma. 2003. "China's urbanization levels: Reconstructing a baseline from the fifth population census." *The China Quarterly* 173: 176–96.

Index